BREAK THROUGH FAST

BREAK THROUGH FAST

ACCESSING THE POWER OF GOD

GUILLERMO MALDONADO

Boldface type in the Scripture quotations indicates the author's emphasis. The forms *Lord* and *God* (in small caps) in Bible quotations represent the Hebrew name for God *Yahweh* (Jehovah), while *Lord* and *God* normally represent the name *Adonai*, in accordance with the Bible version used.

Cover Design: Caroline Pereira

Breakthrough Fast: ***Accessing the Power of God***

Guillermo Maldonado
14100 SW 144th Ave. • Miami, FL 33186
King Jesus Ministry / ERJ Publicaciones
www.kingjesus.org / www.ERJPub.org

ISBN: 978-1-64123-165-7 • eBook ISBN: 978-1-64123-169-5
Printed in the United States of America

Whitaker House
1030 Hunt Valley Circle • New Kensington, PA 15068
www.whitakerhouse.com

Library of Congress Cataloging-in-Publication Data (pending)

1 2 3 4 5 6 7 8 9 10 11 12 **W** 26 25 24 23 22 21 20 19 18

CONTENTS

PREFACE: RECEIVE WITH EXPECTATION!

I anticipate God working in remarkable ways as you read and apply this book to your life. You may be new to fasting, or you may already have begun to make fasting a regular part of your lifestyle. Either way, you will come to realize that...

- Fasting is not about depriving yourself but about expanding your ability to receive and release the presence and power of the Spirit.
- Fasting is not about being physically hungry but about being spiritually hungry for God so you can be filled with the life that truly satisfies.
- Fasting is not about losing out on what is natural but about gaining what is supernatural.

I can testify to the power of fasting—so many breakthroughs that I have seen in my personal life, ministry, and finances have come through prayer and fasting. For this reason, I ask that you receive this teaching with *expectation*. Expectation comes from doing what the Bible asks us to do. If you do your part, you can expect God to act on your behalf—not as "payment" but as a gift of His grace and power. Expect God to transform you and use you as a vessel of His supernatural power as you learn how to enter into a *Breakthrough Fast*.

INTRODUCTION: TIMES OF RESTORATION

Spiritual Power in Fasting

If today's believers only knew the spiritual power in fasting, they would practice it more! Many people do not understand what fasting means to God and what it can accomplish in their lives. There is a strong emphasis on fasting in the Word of God. There are also many examples of the power of fasting in the lives of believers from early times up to the present. But today, the body of Christ has largely disregarded fasting. This is one reason why there is a lack of power in the church as a whole—with few miracles, signs, healings, deliverances, and other manifestations of the supernatural to transform lives.

Why has fasting essentially been abandoned by God's people? There are various reasons. One cause is our overscheduled lives;

we pack so much into each day that we often neglect important priorities. Another is simply a lack of motivation. But I think one of the most significant reasons is the pervasiveness of a "hyper-grace" outlook in the church. This perspective says that since Christ has redeemed us and conquered Satan, there is nothing we need to contribute to our spiritual growth and safeguarding. But this is not what Jesus teaches us!

If today's believers only knew the spiritual power in fasting, they would practice it more!

It is true that we can freely receive all the benefits Christ won for us on the cross. However, we must appropriate His provision by faith and apply it to all aspects of our lives. And we have a responsibility as God's priests to offer Him spiritual sacrifices of prayer and fasting in order to further His purposes in the world—and in our own lives. (We will discuss these topics in more detail in coming chapters.) We must return to God's original intent for the church—becoming a people who can manifest His love and power in the world. The only way we can do this is to return to both prayer and fasting.

Our Need to Fast and Pray Has Intensified

Additionally, at this time in human history, we are living in the midst of upheaval and revolution—both in the natural world and in the spiritual sphere. As the second coming of the Lord draws near, we are dealing with demonic powers that have never before been seen on the earth. Our need to pray and fast has intensified, because only by these means can we be prepared to confront and overcome these destructive forces of the enemy.

In accordance with this, we are living in the prophetic "*times of restoration of all things*":

> *Repent therefore and be converted, that your sins may be blotted out, so that times of refreshing may come from the presence of the Lord, and that He may send Jesus Christ, who was preached to you before, whom heaven must receive* ***until the times of restoration of all things****, which God has spoken by the mouth of all His holy prophets since the world began.* (Acts 3:19–21)

The word *restoration* means "a bringing back to a former position or condition." It indicates being returned to original intent. In these last days, God wants to restore the church's intimate relationship with Him and empowerment in His Spirit so we can complete His purposes—spreading the gospel of the kingdom throughout the world, bringing salvation, healing, deliverance, and abundance. This restoration includes a stirring in the church to return to living by the Spirit—no longer relying on our own strength and techniques for serving God—and to prepare for the second coming of Jesus Christ.

The book of the prophet Joel describes the end-time restoration of all things, which involves both Israel and the church. In chapters 1 and 2, the prophet describes the desolation of Israel and calls for repentance and fasting. Then, toward the end of chapter 2, we read this word from the Lord about restoration: *"I will restore to you the years that the swarming locust has eaten, the crawling locust, the consuming locust, and the chewing locust, my great army which I sent among you"* (Joel 2:25). The third and final chapter of Joel deals with God judging the nations and blessing His people.

The "*times of restoration of all things*" include a return to prayer and fasting.

What is our responsibility in God's plans for restoration? The promises of God require our personal cooperation—by prayer and fasting. Again, fasting is an essential tool for being empowered by the Spirit; it will enable us to experience breakthroughs in the spiritual realm, especially as we incorporate it as an integral part of our lifestyle. As I wrote in my book *Breakthrough Prayer,* "with a breakthrough, what we need is brought from the spiritual world to the natural world, so that we can see it in a visible or tangible demonstration of God's power or provision." This principle of the necessity of prayer and fasting applies not only to restoration on a global scale but also to restoration in our individual lives, right now, by God's power and provision—in our personal life, marriage, family, finances, ministry, and anything else that needs to be healed, repaired, or given new life.

Prayer and Fasting as a Way of Life

In *Breakthrough Fast,* you will discover how fasting gives you access to the presence of God. This book provides life-changing revelation from God's Word and many personal testimonies about the power of fasting. You will learn what, exactly, fasting is; different types of fasts and their benefits; how to fast effectively; how to obtain and increase spiritual power through fasting; and specific guidelines and steps to make fasting part of your lifestyle. The value of fasting is incalculable—for your relationship with God and for His purposes in the world. Make it a way of life starting today. Jesus said, *"Your Father who sees* [your fasting] *in secret will reward you openly"* (Matthew 6:18).

1

INTRODUCTION TO FASTING

Fasting is one of the keys to entering the presence of God because it enables us to focus exclusively on our relationship with Him. One time, after I had worshipped God for a full hour, I sensed something inside me I'd never felt before. So I said to the Lord, "It feels like something heavy has come on me, something I can't describe. What is it?" He answered, "An inflow of power came into your spirit." I replied, "What do You mean? I didn't You ask for it." He said, "You don't have to ask when you have a close relationship with Me."

From the time God created human beings, He has desired to be one with us in relationship. Our communion with Him mirrors the marriage relationship as He designed it to be, in which couples are united as one flesh. In the church today, many believers lack a close, strong, continual relationship with the Lord where they can receive His life in an ongoing way. The result? *No relationship, no power.*

The spiritual reality is this: before God will commit His power to us, He requires us to be in relationship with Him.

Unless we understand that our entire Christian life centers on our oneness with the Lord, we will not have access to His supernatural power. *All* aspects of His power come through our union with Him. We can't have an outflow of power if we are spiritually immature, uninformed, dry, or stagnant in our relationship with God. For this reason, I always seek to maintain within me a spiritual atmosphere, a spiritual activity, which I receive through ongoing fellowship with the heavenly Father.

The spiritual reality is this: before God will commit His power to us, He requires us to be in relationship with Him.

A Present and Ongoing Relationship

When we receive Jesus as our Savior and Lord, we make a commitment to give our life to God. But we must realize this is only the beginning of our relationship with the Father. It doesn't stop there. Think about your close human relationships: To maintain them, don't you have to invest in them with a commitment of love, time, and other resources? What do you bring to your current relationships? Are you a giver, or only a taker? When we have a relationship with God in which we minister to Him as well as receive from Him—a relationship that is present and ongoing—we will always have access to a wellspring of spiritual strength and power.

All of us as believers are called to seek a deeper, more profound, progressive, continuous, and intense relationship with our heavenly Father—pursuing Him with all our hearts and being filled with His Spirit. Let us be thirsty and hungry for Him, closely aligning ourselves with His will and receiving fresh revelation and knowledge from Him according to His Word. As we grow closer to our heavenly Father, we will become more and more fruitful and productive for His kingdom.

Residing Power and Active Power

When God told me about the inflow of power He had given me during worship, He also said, "There was just an inflow of power; now, you need to get the flow out of you." The inflow was not for my benefit alone but for the purpose of ministering His power to others. If you are a believer, you already have God's power within you through the indwelling Holy Spirit. That is what we call God's "residing power." Then, as you honor the Lord and worship Him, putting Him first in your life by prayer, fasting, and obedience, He will stir up that power within you. That is His "active power"—and His active power must then be released.

Our relationship with God initiates various types of active power, including authority power and miracle-working power. For example, Matthew 10:1 says, "*And when* [Jesus] *had called His twelve disciples to Him, He gave them power over unclean spirits, to cast them out, and to heal all kinds of sickness and all kinds of disease.*" The Greek word translated "*power,*" exousia, generally refers to authority power, or the legal right to exercise power. Such power can only come by virtue of a genuine relationship with God.

Acts 1:8 says, "*You shall receive power when the Holy Spirit has come upon you; and you shall be witnesses to Me in Jerusalem, and in all Judea and Samaria, and to the end of the earth."* Here, the Greek word translated *"power," dunamis,* refers to miracle-working power, which is activated by faith. Our praying and fasting, in themselves, don't release such power, but our faith releases the inflow of power that comes through prayer and fasting in the presence of God.

Thus, even though we all have God's "residing" power, due to the Holy Spirit living within us, we still need to learn to appropriate the power so that it is stirred up and can flow out of us to do God's will and meet the many needs in the world around us. Here we come back to the heart of the matter: the residing power becomes activated by *relationship.* Moreover, a continuing relationship with our Father leads to *continual active power.*

Our faith releases the inflow of power that comes through prayer and fasting in the presence of God.

The Law of Exchange

In our divine relationship with the Father, the "law of exchange" is in operation, in which we receive all that God has for us. This includes an exchange of *name, will,* and *strength.* First, we receive a new name: We belong to God now and are counted as part of His family. (See, for example, 1 John 3:1.) We have also been granted the authority to use the name of His beloved Son Jesus to carry out His purposes. (See, for example, Mark 16:17.) Second, we receive a new will. When our spirit is renewed, God writes His commandments on our hearts. (See, for example, Hebrews 10:16.) Third, we receive new strength—His Spirit lives inside us as an ongoing source of comfort, guidance, and power. (See, for example, John 14:26; Acts 1:8.)

The elements of a full relationship with God are love; obedience; reverence, also called "the fear of the Lord" (see, for example, Deuteronomy 6:2; Psalm 25:14); and commitment. We must continually keep in mind that our relationship with our heavenly Father is based on covenant—and covenant always involves commitment. Psalm 50:5 says, *"Gather My saints together to Me, those who have made a covenant with Me by sacrifice."* We will talk more in coming chapters about this crucial element of sacrifice in fasting. For now, let us focus on the sacrifice Jesus made for us on the cross. Because He died in our place, we enter into a new covenant with God—a covenant of forgiveness for our sins, eternal life, and full access to His presence through Jesus Christ. Our part—our response—to this new covenant is to remain in close fellowship with the Father.

God doesn't give His power to strangers, but only to those who are committed to Him—those who love, obey, and honor Him. As you commit to the Father, You become increasingly one in mind and spirit with Him, so that you begin to speak, talk, and act like Him. As you develop that relationship, God will commit to You in a deeper way and release more of His power in your life. He will reveal to you His will and manifest your spiritual inheritance.

In such a close, committed relationship with the Lord, you will be able to demonstrate His power, according to the Spirit's direction, whenever you see a need. You won't have to wait for "special anointing" because you will appropriate the power of that relationship to heal the sick, cast out demons, and do miracles, signs, and wonders.

Our relationship with our heavenly Father is based on covenant—and covenant always involves commitment.

Fasting and Relationship

Fasting is a vital part of the process of maintaining an ongoing relationship with our heavenly Father because it enables us to deepen our communion with Him, resulting in greater intimacy and power. During a fast, we purposefully designate periods of time when we put aside everything else for the sole purpose of seeking the Lord. We do not engage in other responsibilities or obligations, entertainment, work, or even food in order to put God first and seek His face. As we do this, we see our lives and the lives of others transformed. Sin and temptations are overcome, family members come to Christ, "mountains" are moved, and spiritual power is activated to overcome "impossibilities"!

Many Christians are oppressed, afflicted, sick, depressed, fearful, and lonely. Where is the power in their lives to overcome these conditions? If we lack spiritual power in any area of our lives, then we either do not have a close relationship with God, we do not understand how to activate the power within us, or there are areas we still need to surrender to Him. We can't exercise spiritual power and authority by our own intelligence or according to our own willpower. We need God's power to overcome temptation and to defeat the attacks of the enemy.

All of us have various kinds of difficulties. Some of our troubles may be the result of sin. But we must also remember that we are in a continual spiritual war with the enemy. In both cases, if we lack a vital relationship with the Lord, we won't have the power we need for victory. We also need power to "[bring] *every thought into captivity to the obedience of Christ*" (2 Corinthians 10:5) so that we can live on *"every word that proceeds from the mouth of God"* (Matthew 4:4). We can't just have head knowledge that the Bible says we are to take our thoughts captive. We must be able to exercise that power, and we can do so only from our position of relationship.

The deeper the relationship, the deeper the power. From now on, seek to do everything in your Christian life out of your relationship with the Lord, and not according to your own ability. It takes the power of God to remove mountains and address the issues in our lives relating to our marriages, finances, health, fears, or anything else.

Fasting enables us to deepen our communion with God, resulting in greater intimacy and power.

An Inflow of God's Power

Remember that every time a believer develops a close, personal, continual, progressive relationship with God, there will be an inflow of His power. Casual believers don't produce power.

Ephesians 3:20 says, "[God]...*is able to do exceedingly abundantly above all that we ask or think,* ***according to the power that works in us.***" Again, such active, working power within us comes by virtue of relationship. The power works when there is an inflow. When was the last time you spent time in God's presence and received an inflow of His power?

As you pray and fast, God will deposit His power in you. I have found that the more of God's presence we carry, the faster the power will be activated and released; the more we pray, the more quickly miracles will manifest. We see this pattern in Jesus's life. He continually spent time in the presence of God, and when He went out to minister, the power fell.

If you would like to commit or recommit to having close and continual relationship with the heavenly Father, pray this prayer out loud:

> Father God, I come to You in the name of Your Son Jesus Christ, my Savior. I honor You as God Almighty, and I acknowledge that I stand in Your presence. I repent for neglecting to develop a close relationship with You. Forgive me for having departed from the practices of prayer and fasting, which enable me to build and maintain our relationship. Right now, I commit myself to love You, to obey You, and to serve You by doing Your will. I return to You wholeheartedly. I desire to seek Your face in prayer and fasting. Please give me the power to sustain and deepen my relationship with You. You are my all in all! In Jesus's name, amen.

Testimonies of Breakthrough Fasts

My name is Maria Angelica Sherman. When I was growing up in the Bahamas, I was always considered "daddy's little girl" in a family that was close. However, when I was about ten years old, my parents had an argument. I remember my dad packing his bags and leaving. When this happened, I was very hurt, but later I also felt abandoned and rejected because I never really saw him afterward; he never came to see me.

About eight years ago, I came to the United States, and I was going through a very rough time. This time, my dad left everything in the Bahamas to be with me. When he came here, I felt like I had forgiven him. But there was just something that did not allow me to love him the way I wanted to.

I started attending King Jesus Ministry, and it felt like I had found a home. I had an encounter with the love of God as a Father, and God ministered to me. I learned what it meant to harbor unforgiveness, resentment, and bitterness. When I recognized them for what they were, I was delivered from them and set free. But what God did afterward was beyond compare. My father came to me, opened up his heart, and asked me to forgive him. And that gave closure to everything I had been going through.

I continued going to King Jesus Ministry and serving, and my dad gave his life to Christ. But then a lot of opposition began. We had many financial problems due to the fact that my dad lost his job right at the point he became a Christian. The enemy started to attack my relationship with my mom, because I was defending my dad. I was getting attacked during the very time I had decided to come to church and commit to God. As a result, my mother and I grew apart. But I gave our relationship to God, and she ended up giving her life to Christ, too. She came to me and said, "Daughter, forgive me for the attacks, for coming against you in this time," and God restored our relationship. Then, after I went on a twenty-one-day fast, my sister was saved, as well, and the Lord restored our relationship. We have the most beautiful relationship that you could imagine. The Lord really came into my life and transformed me as an individual and as a daughter of God.

Maria is now an ordained deacon at King Jesus Ministry, helping to restore other people's relationships, including those of marriages and families!

2

WHAT FASTING REALLY IS

What Fasting Is—and *Isn't*

When we see how vital it is to have a deep and ongoing relationship with God, we can understand the true nature of fasting. Here is a good foundational definition of fasting:

> Fasting is the free-will abstinence from food for spiritual purposes—to seek God's presence and deepen one's relationship with Him.

Contrary to the way some people practice it, spiritual fasting is not:

- The avoidance of food to lose weight (though weight loss may be a result)
- A "strategy" or manipulation to get God to do something in particular for us

- A means to draw attention to ourselves and show how "spiritual" we are

We need to fast with the right motives in order to gain the spiritual benefits. In the prophet Isaiah's day, the Israelites fasted, but for selfish reasons and in the wrong way:

> [The Lord declared], *"Why have we fasted," they say, "and You have not seen? Why have we afflicted our souls, and You take no notice?" In fact, in the day of your fast you find pleasure, and exploit all your laborers. Indeed you fast for strife and debate, and to strike with the fist of wickedness. You will not fast as you do this day, to make your voice heard on high.* (Isaiah 58:3–4)

Fasting should not be engaged in unless it is for the purpose of seeking God in prayer at a greater level. That doesn't mean we can't go to God with our needs and requests. Yet the *primary* purpose of fasting is to seek God Himself and His will, receiving His revelation of what He wants to do in our lives and in the lives of others.

We need to fast with the right motives to gain the spiritual benefits.

Many people think that fasting is optional because they don't understand its transforming power and results. Fasting is not an option—it is a necessity. Every believer is called to fast. In fact, it is one of the marks of a true disciple of Jesus Christ.

Some Christians have been taught that we don't have to fast because Jesus paid the sacrifice for us, and we are no longer under law but under grace. However, this is not an issue of law versus grace. Those who take this view will have to explain themselves to the apostles and to Jesus Himself, who taught His disciples to fast! God's people are instructed to fast not only in the Old Testament, but also in the New Testament.

During Jesus's earthly ministry, He was asked, "*Why do the disciples of John* [the Baptist] *and of the Pharisees fast, but Your disciples do not fast?*" (Mark 2:18). It appeared on the surface that fasting was not part of Jesus's lifestyle or teachings. But as we will see in this chapter and the next, that was not the case. Jesus gave specific guidelines for fasting in a way that is pleasing to God. So what was Jesus's response to this question?

> *Can the friends of the bridegroom fast while the bridegroom is with them? As long as they have the bridegroom with them they cannot fast. But the days will come when the bridegroom will be taken away from them, and then they will fast in those days.* (verses 19–20)

Fasting is not an option—it is a necessity. It is one of the marks of a true disciple of Jesus Christ.

Jesus is the Bridegroom. Therefore, while the disciples were continually with Him, they did not need to fast. However, from the time Jesus ascended to heaven after His resurrection, the church—the bride of Christ—has practiced fasting. We will not fast after Jesus returns for His bride because we will be with Him forever (see 1 Thessalonians 4:16–17); but for now, fasting is to be an integral part of our lives.

When Should We Fast?

Throughout Scripture, we see how God's people sought His presence through prayer and fasting. Sometimes, God ordained or urged a particular fast for His people; other times, individuals, groups, or nations instigated a fast due to a need. Thus, a breakthrough fast is initiated in one of two ways: The first is when God specifically calls His people (whether a group or an individual) to a fast in order to return to Him and His ways or to intercede for a specific issue. This is referred to as a "sovereign fast." The second is when a believer originates a fast for a particular purpose. This is called "fasting by faith." In both types of fasting, we need to rely on the Holy Spirit for guidance and strength.

The Sovereign Fast

One biblical example of God calling His people to a fast is found in the book of Joel: "*'Now, therefore,' says the Lord, 'turn to Me with all your heart, with fasting, with weeping, and with mourning*'" (Joel 2:12). The Hebrew word translated "*turn*" means to return to the point of departure. God wanted the Israelites to return to a close relationship with Him. He also wanted them to represent Him accurately to other nations whose people did not know Him. Previous to this exhortation, the prophet Joel had proclaimed, "*Consecrate a fast, call a sacred assembly; gather the elders and all the inhabitants of the land into the house of the* Lord *your God, and cry out to the* Lord" (Joel 1:14).

Today, God may prompt a pastor or another leader to declare a fast for a congregation or group. Or, He may call an individual believer to a fast, giving them the desire and will to enter into it, and the grace to complete it. As Paul wrote, "*For it is God who works in you both to will and to do for His good pleasure*" (Philippians 2:13). For example, one day, you might get up in the morning feeling hungry but also with a special desire in your heart to seek God. You will discern that the Holy Spirit is prompting you to fast, and, sometimes, that feeling of hunger will cease. God may or may not reveal His divine purpose for the fast. However, at times, you will discern a specific reason for it. It might be for the purpose of interceding for a particular person, issue, or world event. In those cases, it is a privilege to be chosen by God for such an assignment.

When the Lord leads us to fast, we need to respond. Keep in mind that this will be a *conviction* to fast by the Holy Spirit, which means there will be no guilt, pressure, or condemnation connected with it. Allow God's Spirit to lead you into the fasts He has for you. Learn to hear and obey His voice.

Fasting by Faith

As noted above, this kind of fast is initiated by a believer or believers. Here are some significant reasons for entering into such a fast, which I expand on in this book.

- *To seek the presence of God*. We discussed this primary purpose in chapter 1.

- *To humble ourselves before God.* All believers need to regularly humble themselves before the heavenly Father in acknowledgment of His sovereignty and greatness—and fasting is one of the foundational ways by which we submit our lives to Him. *"Therefore humble yourselves under the mighty hand of God, that He may exalt you in due time"* (1 Peter 5:6). True humbleness is the path to spiritual power because humility always draws God, while pride repels Him. We need to recognize that without the Lord, we are nothing. (See, for example, John 15:5.) Humility before God is a sign of total dependence on Him.

- *To appropriate God's presence,* or to bring God's presence into the environment of a place or situation to allow Him to sovereignly work.

- *To be prepared to respond to the times in which we are living.* We are living in times when satanic forces are influencing all parts of our society. *"But know this, that in the last days perilous times will come"* (2 Timothy 3:1). We are confronting greater sicknesses, corruptions, bondages, discord, and hopelessness than ever before. We need to pray to conquer these maladies in the world. Additionally, as I wrote in the introduction to this book, dangerous demonic entities have entered the world that we have not previously battled, and we need to be ready to counteract them through the power of God.

- *To seek God's direction and guidance.* When we don't know which way to go or when we have several options before us, fasting is a way of pursuing God's will for ourselves, our marriage, our family, our finances, and so on. As the Ezra the priest and scribe wrote, "*Then I proclaimed a fast there at the river of Ahava, that we might humble ourselves before our God, to seek from Him the right way for us and our little ones and all our possessions*" (Ezra 8:21).

- *To receive power for ministry or for handling a certain situation.* For miracles and deliverances to occur, we need a spiritual atmosphere. Fasting brings us into a place in the Spirit where we see new spiritual activity within us and can carry that atmosphere wherever we go. Without spiritual activity, we will operate in the flesh—and the flesh will never produce a miracle.
- *To deal with a crisis.* When we face a current or imminent crisis, we can appeal to God through prayer and fasting. This is what Queen Esther and the exiled Hebrews did when they faced the threat of annihilation. (See Esther 4.)
- *To overcome an impossibility.* Jesus said, "*With men it is impossible, but not with God; for with God all things are possible*" (Mark 10:27).
- *To consecrate and set apart oneself to God for His purposes.* Through fasting, we can offer ourselves as a living sacrifice to God, asking Him to work His complete will in our lives.
- *To activate spiritual gifts and callings.* Fasting cultivates the anointing in our lives. There are gifts within us that are dormant, but when we fast, these gifts are stirred up in us.

- *To receive a specific breakthrough in our lives*—whether physical, mental, emotional, or spiritual. There are some hindrances or delays in our lives that won't change or shift until we fast and pray.

Whenever we enter into a fast by faith, let us keep in mind that fasting changes *us*, not God. God does not need to change! Fasting by faith is a way of showing God our hunger for Him. When He sees our hunger, He will respond to us because of our commitment and persistence; He will transform us and intervene in our situations. Again, fasting is not "paying the price" for God to hear us, because the sacrifice has already been paid by Jesus on the cross. Fasting is for the purpose of sharpening our spiritual focus and perception so we can receive all that Jesus paid for us.

Fasting changes us, not God.
God does not need to change!

One Old Testament example of fasting by faith is the fast initiated by the prophet Daniel for the restoration of the Israelites to their land:

> *In the first year of Darius the son of Ahasuerus, of the lineage of the Medes, who was made king over the realm of the Chaldeans—in the first year of his reign I, Daniel, understood by the books the number of the years specified by the word of the* Lord *through Jeremiah the prophet, that He would accomplish seventy years in the desolations of*

> *Jerusalem. Then I set my face toward the Lord God to make request by prayer and supplications, with fasting, sackcloth, and ashes.* (Daniel 9:1–3)

In the New Testament, Jesus taught His disciples to fast by faith, and we can clearly see how vital fasting was in His own life. Jesus didn't confront and overcome the great temptations by Satan in the desert until, being filled with the Spirit, He was engaged in a lengthy fast—after which He began His ministry empowered by the Holy Spirit.

> *Then Jesus, being filled with the Holy Spirit, returned from the Jordan* [after His baptism] *and was led by the Spirit into the wilderness, being tempted for forty days by the devil. And in those days He ate nothing, and afterward, when they had ended, He was hungry.... Now when the devil had ended every temptation, he departed from Him until an opportune time. Then Jesus returned in the power of the Spirit to Galilee, and news of Him went out through all the surrounding region.* (Luke 4:1–2, 13–14; see also Matthew 4:1–11; Mark 1:12–13)

The Holy Spirit led Jesus to confront the enemy in the wilderness, and Jesus's corresponding fast may have been either a sovereign fast or a fasting by faith. Either way, as an act of His will, in consecration, Jesus presented His body before God in fasting. Before He dealt with the enemy, He needed to be spiritually ready. Many of us are currently confronting the enemy in a particular crisis or an ongoing battle. If this is your situation, have you stopped for a moment and recognized, "I can't overcome this unless I go into a period of fasting"?

Jesus was the purest and holiest Person to walk the face of the earth. He had no sin, yet, as a human being, He still needed to pray and fast in order to defeat the enemy, know the Father's will, and firmly establish His ministry on earth. How much more do we need to pray and fast! We have been wonderfully redeemed by Christ and given the gift of the Holy Spirit. Even so, we still battle against the sinful nature, which continually tries to reassert authority over our lives (see, for example, Romans 7:22–25), and, sadly, we have a tendency to drift away from a close relationship with God. Additionally, we require ongoing power for ministry. As we fast and pray in God's presence, He provides us with wisdom, strength, and anointing.

As I wrote earlier, Jesus gave His disciples instructions about fasting, and we will look at those teachings in coming chapters. (See Matthew 6:16–18; 17:14–21.) We see additional examples of fasting in the New Testament. The biblical record shows that the believers in the early church practiced fasting as an important part of their lifestyle. For example, the prophets and teachers of the church in Antioch prayed and fasted, after which they received a specific word from the Holy Spirit about the ministry of Paul and Barnabas. (See Acts 13:1–3.)

Furthermore, we read in 2 Corinthians that Paul fasted often. (See 6:4–5; 11:27.) Paul wrote about half of the books in the New Testament, and he was probably the greatest apostle of all time—and yet he felt the need to regularly fast. The most powerful men and women of God from earliest times until today have followed a lifestyle of prayer and fasting.

Fasting was vital to the life and ministry of Jesus. The same holds true for His followers today.

What Forms Does Fasting Take?

Fasting takes two main forms: partial fasts and total fasts.

A Partial Fast

This form of fast is partial with regard to either the time frame committed to it or the specific foods that are abstained from. For example, you might fast one or two meals a day. Or, you might eat three meals a day but not eat certain foods you especially enjoy, such as sweets, carbohydrates, or meat. For a notable example of a partial fast for the spiritual purpose of honoring God, we return to the book of Daniel. Daniel and his friends were among the Israelites carried off to captivity by the invading Babylonian army. They ate only vegetables in order to avoid meat and drink offered to the idols of Babylon, and God honored this fast by giving them favor with their captors. (See Daniel 1.)

A Total Fast

This form of fast is the total and complete elimination of food for a specific period of time (twenty-four hours or more).

It can be done in two ways: not eating food and ingesting only water, or completely eliminating all foods and liquids. The latter is not recommended because the human body is comprised of 80 percent water, and a prolonged abstinence from water could produce serious negative effects. (The instances of such fasts in the Bible were unique circumstances.) Personally, I fast two days a week, either partially or totally. At other times, I fast for three, seven, or twenty-one days at a time. It is essential to seek the guidance of the Holy Spirit when determining the type of fast you will engage in.

A Call to Fasting and Prayer

I believe that, in these days, God is calling His church to return to fasting and prayer. It is one of the pillars that sustain our lives and ministries. Many men and women of God today are not spiritually alert because they have stopped praying and fasting. They have lost their fire and passion for God, for prayer, and for the salvation of souls. God is bringing us back to our first love (see Revelation 2:4–5) so we may regain our edge in the spiritual realm and walk in the power of the Spirit.

Are you ready to begin or renew the practice of fasting? Are you willing to sacrifice food for one or more days in order to seek the Lord? Many of the world's religions include fasting among their practices. How much more should we as Christians fast in order to honor and obey the living God! You will experience breakthroughs in your life when you make fasting and praying a regular part of your lifestyle.

If you would like to be part of this renewal of prayer and fasting, please pray this prayer out loud:

> Heavenly Father, I ask You to give me the grace to incorporate fasting and prayer into my lifestyle. I am among those who have lost my passion for You and for ministering to others in Your name. I want to seek Your face. I want to advance Your kingdom. Thank You for calling me to a deeper relationship with You and filling me with Your Spirit so I can regain my spiritual perception and be used as a vessel for Your kingdom purposes. In Jesus's name, amen!

Testimonies of Breakthrough Fasts

My name is Petrus Mashwele Mokgwaui, and I am from the villages of Strydkraal Limpopo, a province of South Africa. I am twenty-three years old, and I am a nurse and science student. I grew up going to church, but it was in an atmosphere where I did not know anything about the supernatural, and neither did my father, who was the pastor. We did not know that there was more to church than just a religious structure. There were only eight members in our church. My father would preach, but there were no supernatural manifestations of the Holy Spirit and the power of God. We saw no miracles or casting out of demons.

While I was in my third year of college studying nursing, I was at the mall in my town and came across some of the teachings and other material on the supernatural by Apostle Maldonado. I felt a pull and a desire to know what the supernatural was, so I started reading one of his books. During the first three days, I couldn't understand why I was reading content that talked about how reason and doubt had replaced the supernatural. For example, my studies in nursing told me that HIV cannot be healed and that the dead cannot be resurrected. But the teachings of the supernatural say the opposite—that miracles, signs, and wonders are evident and possible today.

I decided to go on a twenty-one-day fast because I wanted God to reveal to me the power of the supernatural; I wanted to have an encounter with the Holy Spirit so He would make known spiritual things to me. During the fast, I started encountering God and understanding His call. I spoke to my father and told him I was learning about the supernatural and that we needed to allow the Holy Spirit to have room and freedom in our church services!

My father allowed me to preach at the Resurrection Sunday service the following month. I taught on the supernatural, revealing to our church members that God is a God of miracles and that the infilling of the Holy Spirit is necessary. I called those who needed a touch from God or a creative miracle to come to the front. One woman came forward, and the Spirit of God came upon me, and I began to prophesy, "There was something removed from you, an organ...." And she said, "Yes, I had an operation three years ago, and both of my fallopian tubes were removed. As a result, it is impossible for me to get pregnant or bear children." I told her that God was about to create new fallopian tubes for her, and that as evidence, she would bear a beautiful, healthy child. The Holy Spirit spoke this witness through me, the woman believed and had faith, and I declared the creation of new fallopian tubes. The woman came back to our church service the following month testifying of this creative miracle—she was pregnant! She later gave birth to a healthy boy.

The natural, which is based on human reason, intelligence, and wisdom, has replaced the supernatural. It does not speak about the ability of the power of God. Whereas my training in nursing taught me that certain situations could not be changed, I have seen firsthand that the supernatural is the highest reality; it solves impossibilities. When the supernatural manifests, it contradicts the laws of reason and nature. In no way can human reasoning be compared with the supernatural, because the supernatural is above nature!

3

THE THREEFOLD CORD: FASTING, GIVING, AND PRAYING

In coming chapters, I will discuss more specifically what to expect during a fast. But first let us look at Jesus's teachings in Matthew 6 so we can know without any doubt that fasting is meant to be an established part of our walk of faith. To understand this, we need to see the relationship between fasting and two other foundational aspects of our Christian life.

Three Vital Precepts

In the Sermon on the Mount, Jesus revealed three vital precepts—three responsibilities—that apply to every believer: *giving, praying,* and *fasting.* He began by talking about giving offerings:

> *Take heed that you do not do your charitable deeds before men, to be seen by them. Otherwise you have no reward from your Father in heaven. Therefore,* ***when you do a charitable deed,*** *do not sound a trumpet before you as the hypocrites do in the synagogues and in the streets, that they*

> *may have glory from men. Assuredly, I say to you, they have their reward. But* ***when you do a charitable deed,*** *do not let your left hand know what your right hand is doing, that your charitable deed may be in secret; and your Father who sees in secret will Himself reward you openly.*
>
> (Matthew 6:1–4)

Note that Jesus did not say, "*If* you do a charitable deed..." but "*When you do a charitable deed....*" By this statement, Jesus showed that charitable deeds, or acts of giving in various forms, are a normal part of a believer's life, and He explained how that giving should be conducted. Next, Jesus took up the topic of prayer:

> *And* ***when you pray,*** *you shall not be like the hypocrites. For they love to pray standing in the synagogues and on the corners of the streets, that they may be seen by men. Assuredly, I say to you, they have their reward. But you,* ***when you pray,*** *go into your room, and when you have shut your door, pray to your Father who is in the secret place; and your Father who sees in secret will reward you openly. And* ***when you pray,*** *do not use vain repetitions as the heathen do. For they think that they will be heard for their many words. Therefore do not be like them. For your Father knows the things you have need of before you ask Him.*
>
> (Matthew 6:5–8)

After explaining how *not* to pray, Jesus immediately taught the correct way of praying. He gave His disciples a model to follow, which we call the Lord's Prayer. (See verses 9–13.) Again, we see that Jesus didn't say, "*If* you pray..." but "*When you pray....*" He considered prayer to be something every believer would engage in.

Lastly, we see the same pattern in Jesus's instructions about fasting:

> *Moreover, **when you fast**, do not be like the hypocrites, with a sad countenance. For they disfigure their faces that they may appear to men to be fasting. Assuredly, I say to you, they have their reward. But you, **when you fast**, anoint your head and wash your face, so that you do not appear to men to be fasting, but to your Father who is in the secret place; and your Father who sees in secret will reward you openly.*
> (Matthew 6:16–18)

Once more, Jesus didn't say, "*If* you fast..." but "*When you fast....*" Some people think they need to wait for a sign from God or a special feeling before undertaking a fast. Although it's true that God will lead us to enter into sovereign fasts, we can take the initiative to fast at any time. We can make a decision to fast by faith. And as the above teachings from Scripture demonstrate, fasting should be integrated into a believer's regular lifestyle.

Jesus revealed three responsibilities that apply to every believer: *giving*, *praying*, and *fasting*.

Fasting, therefore, is not optional but is expected of Jesus's followers. It is an act of obedience, as well as an excellent means of growing in our relationship with the Father, gaining spiritual strength, and bearing fruit for God.

Motives and Rewards

Jesus exhorted us to examine our motives when participating in either giving, praying, or fasting. To determine if our intentions are pure before the Lord, we need to ask ourselves questions such as these:

- "Which do I want more—applause and rewards from other people or favor and rewards from God?" If we are constantly looking for praise from other people, we will be offended when we fail to obtain from them what we expect to receive. However, if we wait for God's rewards, He will bless us, and we will never be disappointed.
- "What is my reason for giving offerings, praying, or fasting?"
- "Do I always want my work for God to be publicly acknowledged by the pastor or other leaders of my church?"
- "Does it bother me when the amount of money I give is not appreciated or acknowledged?"

Jesus said that what we do for the Father "*in secret*" to honor and serve Him will be rewarded. What will be God's reward for us when we give offerings, pray, and fast for the right reasons? We will have "*treasures in heaven*":

Do not lay up for yourselves treasures on earth, where moth and rust destroy and where thieves break in and steal; but lay up for yourselves treasures in heaven, where neither moth nor rust destroys and where thieves do not break in and steal. For where your treasure is, there your heart will be also.
(Matthew 6:19–21)

We will also receive revelations of God and His Word:

The lamp of the body is the eye. If therefore your eye is good, your whole body will be full of light. (Matthew 6:22)

What we do for the Father "*in secret*" to honor and serve Him will be rewarded.

The Strength of the Threefold Cord

I like to connect these three elements of giving, praying, and fasting with the "*threefold cord*" mentioned in the book of Ecclesiastes:

Though one may be overpowered by another, two can withstand him. And a threefold cord is not quickly broken.
(Ecclesiastes 4:12)

Accordingly, as we serve the Lord, we should focus on each of the elements of this threefold cord:

1. *Giving* is a form of honoring God. To honor means to value, esteem, respect, revere, or consider someone (or something) precious. When we honor our heavenly Father, we do not give to Him out of convenience but according to our love for Him. Honoring God and one's parents (and others) is a sign of spiritual maturity. Honor is also a spiritual currency that is highly rewarded in the kingdom of God. What we do with the first portion, or "firstfruits," of our income (see Proverbs 3:9) will determine what will happen to the rest of it. Will it dry up, will it be void of any spiritual significance—or will it become fruitful and multiply for the kingdom? When we honor God with our giving, He will demonstrate His power and provision in our life in a way we've never seen before. Remember, this is not a "payment" for seeking and honoring Him but rather a response of His love and grace through Jesus Christ.

2. *Prayer* is communication with God. Every relationship is based on communication, and we should continually be in contact with our heavenly Father throughout the day. What is the first thing we communicate to Him? Our worship. Through the Lord's Prayer, Jesus taught that we are to first minister to God when we pray, honoring and praising His name, and aligning ourselves with His will: *"Our Father in heaven, hallowed be Your name. Your kingdom come. Your will be done on earth as it is in heaven"* (Matthew 6:9–10). When you honor God with your worship and praise, you will find that your prayers are answered. If you don't honor God at the beginning

of your "Abba Father" prayer, the rest of the prayer will not be applicable to you. (See verses 11–13.)

3. *Fasting* is presenting our bodies to God as a living sacrifice. We will continue to discuss this theme and its implications in the next chapter.

When we honor God with our giving, He will demonstrate His power and provision in our life in a way we've never seen before.

A Loose Cord?

Many people wonder, "Why am I not receiving answers to my prayers?" Have you felt that way? Could it be that one (or more) of the threefold cords in your spiritual life is loose or frayed? Let us search our hearts to see if we are meeting our responsibilities to give, pray, and fast—seeking the face of God and honoring Him with our whole life. When we do what is right in God's sight, we can defeat our "flesh," or the sinful nature, and the devil through the power of the Spirit. I believe that as you weave together this threefold cord in service to God, you will experience breakthroughs in every area of your life!

If you want your life to come into alignment with the threefold cord, please pray the following prayer:

Heavenly Father, I honor Your name and desire to do Your will. Forgive me for seeking the applause of other people instead of seeking Your favor and eternal rewards. I want to incorporate the threefold cord of giving, praying, and fasting into my life. Please give me the grace to obey You in all areas of my life so I may grow in my knowledge of You, gain spiritual strength, and bear fruit for You. In Jesus's name, amen!

Testimonies of Breakthrough Fasts

My name is Xiomara Antonio, and I am from Angola. When I lived in my native country, I didn't have a relationship with God. However, my father is a pastor, so I did know about God, and I knew that He is able to do miracles.

I came to the United States as an international student, majoring in marketing, with a minor in accounting. My parents were not with me, and I didn't have anyone to depend on besides God. I needed a strong relationship with Him. I used to go to another church, but when I started attending King Jesus Ministry, I really felt like I was home. I learned many things about prayer and fasting, and it helped me a lot in my walk with God. I learned I needed to forgive people. For example, I had a lot of grudges against my mother. We have the same personality and therefore we clash a lot. However, through fasting, I learned how I needed to deal with my mother and all the broken relationships in my life.

I fasted during the youth conference at King Jesus Ministry and asked God to deliver a word for me. They called all the youth who were sons and daughters of pastors to come forward for ministry. Someone prophesied over me that I would receive a scholarship. At that very time, I was waiting to hear about a particular scholarship. I'd had no word about it, and I had started to doubt I would receive it. I thought, *Maybe the scholarship is not for me.*

By the end of that year, I was applying to another school because I wanted to transfer from one university to another. To my surprise, the prophetic word that had been released over my life actually came to pass. I was awarded a dean's scholarship of five thousand dollars per school year to attend Nova Southeastern University. I was very surprised because I never thought I would have a scholarship from a source within the US. I always thought that my scholarship would come from my native country. But that was not God's plan. He is amazing. He works in ways we don't expect.

4

APPROPRIATING POWER THROUGH FASTING

In chapter 2, we looked at this foundational definition of fasting:

> Fasting is the free-will abstinence from food for spiritual purposes—to seek God's presence and deepen one's relationship with Him.

In this chapter, we add to that basic definition with these further aspects of what fasting means:

> Fasting is our spiritual sacrifice as priests of the new covenant through Jesus Christ; it is part of our calling in God.

> Fasting is presenting our body as a living sacrifice to God, as an act of our will, for the purpose of consecration and dedication to Him.

God's Kings and Priests

Since ancient times, fasting has been a spiritual sacrifice offered to God by His children. In Christ, all believers have been made *"kings and priests to our God"* (Revelation 5:10; see also Revelation 1:6). As God's priests, we are to present spiritual offerings and sacrifices to the Lord. The apostle Peter wrote:

> *You also, as living stones, are being built up a spiritual house,* ***a holy priesthood, to offer up spiritual sacrifices*** *acceptable to God through Jesus Christ.... You are a chosen generation,* ***a royal priesthood,*** *a holy nation, His own special people, that you may proclaim the praises of Him who called you out of darkness into His marvelous light.*
>
> (1 Peter 2:5, 9)

As a holy and royal priesthood, we are to draw near to God every day, offering sacrifices to Him such as worship, praise, prayer, fasting, and generous giving. In chapter 2 of *Breakthrough Fast,* I mentioned how the leaders of the New Testament church at Antioch *"ministered to the Lord and fasted"* (Acts 13:2). We can actually minister to the Lord as we worship and fast, and these sacrifices become a sweet aroma to Him. (See, for example, Ephesians 5:2.) Fasting is a form of worship because when we sacrifice our normal intake of food, we put our flesh, or the fallen nature, under submission; we prevent it from usurping authority over our spirit. This enables us to put God first in our lives.

Today, a number of Christians know how to minister to other people, and they understand that this ministry is an essential part of serving the Lord. However, they don't know how to minister to God, and they don't realize that this, too, is a vital part of their calling. The church must learn how to minister to God as His priests, offering spiritual sacrifices such as fasting. When we cease eating for the purpose of worshipping and honoring the Lord, seeking first His kingdom, God doesn't take that sacrifice lightly. Remember, *"your Father who sees* [your fasting] *in secret will reward you openly"* (Matthew 6:18).

Today, many believers know how to minister to other people, but they haven't learned how to minister to God.

Consecrating Ourselves to God—Set Apart for His Service

There are many different types of sacrifices we can offer God, but the greatest is the sacrifice of *ourselves*. One of the best ways we can offer this sacrifice is to consecrate our lives, or set ourselves apart, to be dedicated to Him. There are various means by which we approach God and demonstrate we are consecrated to Him, and one of the most effective ways is by prayer and fasting.

Many Christians have not yet entered into such a depth of commitment. They might have experienced God's fire, been a vessel through which He has worked supernatural signs and wonders, and even given tithes and offerings—but they have not yet fully consecrated themselves to God. They have not made it a regular practice to submit to Him. To be consecrated to God means to be totally surrendered and set apart for His exclusive use. We are to be separated and consecrated *to* God and *for* God.

Becoming a Living Spiritual Sacrifice

> *I beseech you therefore, brethren, by the mercies of God, that you present your bodies a living sacrifice, holy, acceptable to God, which is your reasonable service. And do not be conformed to this world, but be transformed by the renewing of your mind, that you may prove what is that good and acceptable and perfect will of God.* (Romans 12:1–2)

When we fast, we present ourselves, including our body, to the Lord as a "*living sacrifice.*" In the Old Testament, under the law, the Israelites followed the practice of regularly bringing sacrifices to the temple in order to have their sins forgiven so they could draw close to God again. The sacrifices were certain animals that had been slain. But under the new covenant, Jesus Christ is our eternal sacrifice. He is "*the Lamb* [of God] *slain from the foundation of the world*" (Revelation 13:8) on our behalf. Consequently, our sacrificial requirement today is to present ourselves *alive* to God in consecration and dedication—and that includes presenting to Him our body.

The body is the outer shell, or dwelling place, of our spirit—our essential, immortal, inner being. It is also the abode of our soul—our mind, will, and emotions. Moreover, the body of a believer is a "*temple*" where the Holy Spirit resides. (See 1 Corinthians 3:16; 6:19.) In Romans 12:1, the expression *"living sacrifice"* refers to worshipping God with all aspects of our being—spirit, soul, and body. Since wholehearted worship takes place where it is offered and expressed through *all* these areas, the body must be presented as a living sacrifice along with the spirit and soul. And a major way we do this is through fasting. Let each one of us make a steadfast decision, through prayer, to regularly present our body to God as a living sacrifice!

Our sacrificial requirement today is to present ourselves alive to God in consecration and dedication—and that includes presenting to Him our body.

Surrendering Our Body

How do we subjugate our body to fast in order to seek God? This is a challenge because the body always wants to follow the desires of the flesh, which are contrary to those of God's Spirit. (See, for example, Romans 7:5; Galatians 5:16–17.) In the Bible, the *"flesh"* is also called *"the old man"* and the *"passions."* (See, for example, Ephesians 4:22; Galatians 5:24.) The flesh never wants to fast because it easily conforms to bad habits and wants to indulge in unrestrained desires—continually craving more food, sex, sleep, and so on. Therefore, when we present our body as a living sacrifice before God, we are not just following a religious doctrine, ritual, or custom. We are, in actuality, consecrating and dedicating our own body to God in total surrender.

Paul tells us that presenting our body to God is a *"reasonable service"* (Romans 12:1). Another translation of this phrase reads:

"reasonable (rational, intelligent) service and spiritual worship" (AMPC). With the requirement to be a living sacrifice, God is not asking us to do something unreasonable or something we can't accomplish. Instead, to offer ourselves in this way is a rational and logical act, based on what He has done for us. We find an excellent explanation of this in *Vine's* dictionary: "The sacrifice is to be intelligent, in contrast to those offered by ritual and compulsion; the presentation is to be in accordance with the spiritual intelligence of those who are new creatures in Christ and are mindful of 'the mercies of God.'"* We surrender our body to God as a conscious decision of our will in gratitude for His mercy and grace in our lives.

Laying Aside Every Weight and Sin

> *Therefore we also, since we are surrounded by so great a cloud of witnesses, let us lay aside every weight, and the sin which so easily ensnares us, and let us run with endurance the race that is set before us.* (Hebrews 12:1)

The *"weight"* mentioned in the above verse refers to any weight that would keep us from winning the *"race"*—any hindrance that would prevent us from staying true to our relationship with God and serving Him wholeheartedly throughout our lives. Accordingly, we could apply the term *weight* to either spiritual, emotional, mental, or physical weights in our lives.

---

* W. E. Vine, Merrill F. Unger, and William White, Jr., *Vine's Complete Expository Dictionary of Old and New Testament Words* (Nashville, TN: Thomas Nelson, Inc., 1996), s.v. "reasonable," 509–510.

These weights block the free flow of God's Spirit. When we carry excess weight, God cannot accelerate His anointing in our lives or unfold many of His purposes for us. (In the next chapter, we will talk more about this factor and how to be set free from these hindrances.) We cannot allow excess weight in any area to keep us from carrying out our responsibilities with excellence. Christian living is a long-distance run of faith and endurance; therefore, to finish it well, our body must become "weightless" and not hold us back.

The apostle Paul learned to place his body under submission and present it as a living and pleasing sacrifice before God. Based on his experience, this is what he instructed the Corinthians:

> *Everyone who competes in the games goes into strict training. They do it to get a crown that will not last, but we do it to get a crown that will last forever. Therefore I do not run like someone running aimlessly; I do not fight like a boxer beating the air. No, I strike a blow to my body and make it my slave so that after I have preached to others, I myself will not be disqualified for the prize.*
>
> (1 Corinthians 9:25–27 NIV)

The reference to "striking a blow" implies the act of disciplining our body into submission. In fasting, this means sacrificing the desire to eat (especially the desire for excessive eating) for a period of time and avoiding taking in anything that might harm the functioning of the body.

Fasting trains us to discipline ourselves. We place constraints on our appetite and desire for food, and in so doing, we develop self-control. Fasting strengthens us to say no to the cravings of the flesh and the temptations of the enemy.

People who practice fasting develop strong discipline.

Maintaining Our Spiritual "Edge"

By offering ourselves as a living sacrifice, we are also enabled to become more spiritually discerning. We identify with God and receive revelation about His nature, will, and purposes. The more spiritually attuned we are, the quicker we will be able to perceive realities in the supernatural realm. When we fast, God begins to sharpen our ability to see, hear, and discern those realities. Thus, fasting helps us not only to gain, but also to maintain, our "edge" in the Spirit, readying us to be used for His purposes.

Many believers have lost their spiritual edge, with the result that they are now functioning more in the natural realm than the spiritual domain. Whenever we lose our edge, our spiritual perceptiveness and authority are weakened, and we start to function like a nominal believer or even like someone who does not believe in God and His power. Fasting brings us into a place in the Spirit where we see new spiritual activity in our life—things we've never seen before. As I discuss more completely in coming chapters, there are certain places in God—realms and dimensions of the Spirit—that we won't have access to unless we fast.

Consecration Brings or Increases the Anointing

Accordingly, when we consecrate ourselves to God as living sacrifices, He brings or increases the anointing in our lives. God has given me a particular commission for ministry: "Called to bring the supernatural power of God to this generation." Therefore, my conviction is that I owe to the world an experience with the power of the living God. When I see various needs, it inspires and prompts me to consecrate myself to God again, so that my spirit, soul, and body will be dedicated to Him—and used by Him in whatever way He desires for me to fulfill this commission.

At one point, I was ministering in Argentina, and there were 27,000 people in the stadium for a meeting. In the midst of this ministry, the Lord said to me, "I want you to do a fast of forty days. What is about to come into your life demands and requires transition, and that is the reason you must fast." There was a time when I didn't understand why anyone would go on a forty-day fast, such as we read about in the Bible. Then I learned that the number forty represents change, renewal, and transition. There are things in our lives that won't shift or change until we fast and pray. God might not require you to do a forty-day fast, but He will guide you into the length of fast He desires in order to bring about the necessary transition for your further spiritual growth, anointing, and service.

Many people today want a shortcut to God's power. They want the power but not the fasting. They want the success but not the sacrifice. But true success in God comes through consecration and surrender. Those who separate themselves to God for the purpose of fasting will come into power. Do you really want more spiritual power? Then, start to regularly fast and pray.

This generation wants a shortcut to power. There are no shortcuts but only surrender and consecration.

Consecration Stirs Up Our Gifts

Since consecration increases the anointing, when we fast, we can also cultivate and stir up God's gifts within us. Paul wrote to Timothy, *"I remind you to stir up the gift of God which is in you through the laying on of my hands"* (2 Timothy. 1:6). The Greek verb translated *"stir up"* in this verse means to "re-enkindle." Another way of looking at it is a reawakening or arousing from sleep.

Is it possible for a person to have the anointing and the gifts of the Holy Spirit but not have spiritual activity in their life? Yes, it is possible. This happens when the gifts and the anointing are dormant, or asleep. If this is the case, they need to be activated. Sometimes, we allow our gifts or anointing to fall dormant, and then we go through a season of dryness and emptiness. By neglecting or rejecting what the Holy Spirit has given us, and not allowing Him to work in our lives, we can *"quench"* Him. (See 1 Thessalonians 5:19.)

There may be spiritual gifts within you that are dormant, or gifts the Lord has released upon you that have yet to be manifested. You need to awaken any dormant places in your spiritual life. It might be that you have areas of giftedness that have never before come to the surface, which the Holy Spirit wants to activate in you. Perhaps you haven't even realized they're there. Or maybe you have neglected to use gifts that you once used regularly. In either of these situations, you can stir up or awaken your anointing by prayer and fasting. When we fast, the gifts within us will begin to be stirred up, including gifts of the Spirit and ministry gifts. (See, for example, 1 Corinthians 12; Ephesians 4:11–12.) God wants us to stir up those gifts!

Fasting is an important way to stir up spiritual gifts in our lives.

Consecration Brings God's Direction

Furthermore, consecrating ourselves to God through fasting prepares the spiritual atmosphere for His Spirit to speak to us and guide us. For example, when you have to make a difficult or important decision and need the Lord's direction, that is a good time to declare a fast by faith and make time to pray and seek the Lord. Fasting increases our sensitivity to God's voice. It enables us to hear His words with greater clarity and certainty.

Consecration Angers the Enemy

Please be aware that when you fast, the enemy will send distractions into your life. He will bring interruptions involving people, places, and things. For example, the day you start fasting, someone might offer you your favorite food! Or, you might get a craving for a certain dish, when you never had a craving for it before. An old friend you haven't seen in a while might suddenly stop by and offer to take you out to lunch. Or, when you begin to pray, you might get several phone calls in a row.

When you experience such distractions, remember that the enemy tried the same thing with Jesus when He fasted and prayed in the wilderness. In Jesus's case, the devil brought temptations to try to prevent Him from remaining in God's presence. The Son of Man overcame these distracting temptations because He was immersed in God's Word and was committed to obeying His heavenly Father. After He had overcome the devil, *"Jesus returned in the power of the Spirit"* (Luke 4:14). He went out to the surrounding areas bringing the kingdom of heaven to earth by healing the sick and casting out demons. (See, for example, Luke 4.)

The devil doesn't want you to pray and fast, either, so he will try to cause you to lose your focus. He knows you will come out of your fast in the power of God, so that your family members will be saved, you will receive deliverance in your mind and emotions, and you will advance in God's purposes for your life. You will come out in the power of God! Now do you understand why Jesus fasted? In a fast, you receive God's power because you are consecrating your body to Him, you're offering yourself to Him, you're ministering to Him—and God responds to this ministry. He sees it as a spiritual sacrifice.

People who are not inclined toward fasting miss out on such manifestations of God's anointing and the many exciting ways in which He desires to spread His kingdom in the world. When I want to increase the anointing in my life, I proclaim a fast and follow it, and the effects are immediate. Miracles and healings occur more quickly. Deliverances are vastly more powerful. These results are a sign that the anointing has increased. All believers need to cultivate the anointing in their lives through fasting. Start waking up spiritual activity in your life now!

Consecration Prepares Believers for Ministry and Leadership

In addition to its importance for the act of personal consecration to God, fasting is significant in the process of consecrating believers in the church for ministry. We saw an example of this earlier with the church at Antioch. Recall how the prophets and teachers of that church prayed and fasted, after which they received a specific word from the Holy Spirit about a new ministry of apostleship for Paul and Barnabas. (See Acts 13:1–3; 14:14.)

Moreover, fasting loosens the impartation to ordain local leaders in the church, which the newly commissioned apostles Paul and Barnabas did as part of their ministry:

> *And when they had preached the gospel to that city and made many disciples, they returned to Lystra, Iconium, and Antioch, strengthening the souls of the disciples, exhorting them to continue in the faith, and saying, "We must through many tribulations enter the kingdom of God." So when they had* ***appointed elders in every church, and prayed with***

> ***fasting,*** *they commended them to the Lord in whom they had believed.* (Acts 14:21–23)

When we fast, therefore, we present and dedicate ourselves to the Lord, ministering to Him with sacrifices of worship, praise, and our very lives. If you would like to consecrate yourself to God, or renew your consecration to Him, begin by praying this prayer:

> Father God, today, I consecrate myself to You. I present my body to You as a living sacrifice as an act of my will, for Your exclusive use. You have my attention, and I will hear and obey You now and in the days to come. I will fast, I will pray, and I will seek Your face. I ask You to give me Your grace to do this faithfully. I want to be Your vessel, used for Your glory. Right now, I am consecrated and dedicated to You. Use me, Lord. In Jesus's name, amen!

Testimonies of Breakthrough Fasts

My name is Carlos, and I grew up in a Christian family in Texas. However, I was not committed to God. In high school, I didn't have a strong role model, and I would go out to parties and drink. I was also addicted to pornography. Then I went to a deliverance retreat at King Jesus Ministry, and God encountered me there. He told me, "You know I am with you! I have always been with you!" He touched me that day and told me not to worry because He would always be there for me.

From that moment, my life turned around. I was freed from all my addictions, and I stopped attending worldly parties and drinking. I began to fall in love with God. I was able to feel His embrace in my deliverance. The Lord had restored my innocence. After I was baptized, I felt an even stronger connection with Him. I had never experienced anything like that!

One day, I was at football practice when someone ran into me and broke my hand. From my wrist to my thumb, the bone was shattered. In the X-ray, my bone looked like a candy cane. My doctors told me I was done for the rest of the year, and that I would need to wear a cast all summer. I would also need surgery. Lastly, I was told I would never be able to play football again.

I told the Lord I needed healing, and I was prayed for, but nothing happened. I struggled with daily activities like writing and showering by myself. I remember watching a video on YouTube, produced by our church, about a guy who had suffered an accident and injured his eye, but God healed him and restored his vision. That testimony made me want my healing even more. I felt I needed to fast all week, so I would eat one meal a day, at noon, and declare healing over my body.

I went to a service at my church, and there was a man there visiting from Germany who asked if he could pray for my hand. When he prayed, I felt my hand grow warm, and I also felt something so amazing in my heart. I decided to take a step of faith, so I took off my cast and touched the bone where my finger had been popped out, and I didn't feel anything! I had received my healing! I was just amazed; I was like, wow! It's unbelievable. I knew that I could receive healing, but I had been skeptical because it hadn't happened right away. When I saw this happen, I knew God was real. I went from living a crazy life to falling in love with God and receiving His healing. He is powerful—and I am speechless.

5

THE RESULTS OF FASTING

Getting Our Attention!

God uses fasting to draw our full attention to Him, which allows Him to work transformation in our life. There are two ways in which this can happen. The process can begin each time we offer ourselves as a living sacrifice to the Lord in a regular practice of fasting. In these times, we purposefully take the focus off our daily concerns so we can listen to His voice. However, God can get our attention even before we start a fast—when we face a difficult situation that drives us to diligently seek Him for answers.

In the book of Hosea, God said of the Israelites, "*I will return again to My place till they acknowledge their offense. Then they will seek My face;* ***in their affliction they will earnestly seek Me***" (Hosea 5:15). A crisis gets our attention, causing us to turn to God. When we are in such a quandary, we feel compelled to recognize, "I must consecrate myself to God and ask for His help. There is no other way to solve this dilemma." Sometimes, we can be so out of spiritual focus due to a preoccupation with "*the cares of this world, the deceitfulness of riches, and the desires for other things*" (Mark 4:19), or because of disobedience to God's Word, that He allows a difficulty to come into our lives. He doesn't send crises, but He uses them to redirect our attention to Him and take us to the next spiritual level while developing Christlike character in us.

An Entrance to the Supernatural

It is human nature to seek God during a time of trouble. Unfortunately, after the affliction ends, we often become complacent again. That is why God sometimes has to keep us continually on our knees before Him. He desires to help us in our situation. However, even more than that, He wants us to understand that He is our only true Source and Deliverer—not only in the midst of a crisis, but at all times.

Accordingly, our entrance into the reality of the supernatural often comes through a difficulty that we are unable to solve. We may never know how powerful and supernatural our God is until we are in dire trouble and receive a miracle from Him in the midst of it. In fact, one of the purposes of miracles is to manifest the nature and power of God. (See, for example, Mark 16:20; Hebrews 2:3–4.)

Yet before showing us His power and provision, God will often use the crisis to change us from the inside out. During a fast, He usually won't reveal Himself to us until He first shows us the needy condition of our heart and where we have strayed from His truths and purposes. That is why the beginning part of a fast is often the hardest—this is the time when God purifies us from our weaknesses and disobedience. These are the spiritual "weights" that slow us down in the long-distance run of our spiritual life, which we talked about in the previous chapter. Let's look at the processes by which God cleanses us, thereby removing these weights from our lives.

Fasting Removes "Contaminations"

When we fast, God removes spiritual "contaminations" from our soul. Our soul needs to be cleansed because, over the course of time, it becomes infected by negative atmospheres. By exposure to the influences of the world (the mind-set hostile or indifferent to God), the soul accumulates spiritual impurities, mixtures of truth and error, and so forth. For instance, we may be contaminated by harboring bitterness or unforgiveness toward a family member or a fellow brother or sister in our church. Or, we may be contaminated by spending a lot of time with people who have negative attitudes, which we pick up, so that we cease reflecting the nature of Christ. God wants to remove these contaminations from us. In fasting, we can surrender all such things to the Lord. (See, for example, James 4:8.)

When we offer our lives to God as a living sacrifice, we commit ourselves to come into agreement with His mind and to be obedient to His will. As we become sensitive to that will, we can align our lives accordingly and become one with God's purposes. We can help keep our soul under the control of our spirit by taking all errant, disobedient thoughts "*into captivity to the obedience of Christ*" (2 Corinthians 10:5). Thus, as we begin to fast, God says to us, in essence, "Before I show Myself to you in answer to what you're looking for, let Me purify you. You need to really see yourself before you see Me."

This requires us to humble ourselves before the presence of God. When we do so, He begins to work in our heart, and we return to living in the light. Prideful people live in the darkness, but humble people live in the light. Humble people also carry God's favor, because His favor is always attached to humility. After humbling our souls in fasting, we gain deeper fellowship with the Father. He cleanses us anew through His Word (see Ephesians 5:25–27) and Spirit, and He sets us apart for Himself once again. We receive His anointing and power, so we can be equipped to serve Him.

During the first part of a fast, God always detoxes and cleanses our souls.

Fasting Crucifies the "Flesh"

Another way we remove spiritual weights from our lives is by "crucifying our flesh." The Scriptures say, "*Those who are Christ's have crucified the flesh with its passions and desires*" (Galatians 5:24). As we discussed in the previous chapter, the "*flesh*" is also referred to as the "old man" or the "passions." Additional terms include the "carnal nature," the "sinful nature," and the "Adamic nature" (in reference to Adam's disobedience to God in the garden of Eden).

Fasting breaks down the power of the flesh in our lives very quickly. That is another reason why the enemy hates it when we begin to fast. He wants us to remain spiritually immature and ineffective. Usually, before we fast, our flesh, rather than our spirit, is more in control of our lives. We need to move out of the natural realm and the operations of the flesh. As we fast and yield to God, He begins to transform us and lift us up. Paul wrote, "*Those who live according to the flesh set their minds on the things of the flesh, but those who live according to the Spirit, the things of the Spirit*" (Romans 8:5), and "*So I say, walk by the Spirit, and you will not gratify the desires of the flesh*" (Galatians 5:16 NIV).

Fasting is God's weapon for dealing with the flesh.

When we are living according to the flesh, we can't perceive spiritual things (a topic we will discuss further in the next chapter of this book). "*The natural man does not receive the things of the Spirit of God, for they are foolishness to him; nor can he know them, because they are spiritually discerned*" (1 Corinthians 2:14). In contrast, when we fast, the Holy Spirit becomes a greater reality to us than anything in the natural world. With a heightened perception of the spiritual realm, the presence of God becomes more real to us. We also become more aware of the enemy and his schemes, and how to deal with them. This enables us to be prepared for whatever difficulties may come our way.

Let me ask you: When a personal crisis looms, which is more real to you—the presence of God's Spirit or the problem? When sickness comes upon you, or you receive a negative report from the doctor, which is more real to you—the power of the Spirit or the illness? When a financial emergency arises, which is more real to you—prosperity in the Spirit or lack?

Fasting puts your flesh under subjection to the Spirit so that the kingdom of God becomes more significant to you than the temporal situations of earth. Your fasting communicates to your flesh, in effect, "Be quiet! I won't listen to you. You don't dictate to me—you are not my master; you are my servant." As the Holy Spirit begins to take control of your life, you become more spiritually oriented and attuned, and this is reflected in your thoughts, words, and actions.

Therefore, until the Holy Spirit and the life of God become our greatest reality, the flesh will dominate us. We will think, act, and react according to the "old man." The evidence of our death to self is that we have come under submission to Christ. This evidence manifests, for example, when an angry, discouraged, or fearful person, after having yielded to God, begins to live in the freedom of life in Christ, exhibiting the fruit of the Spirit: *"the fruit of the Spirit is love, joy, peace, longsuffering, kindness, goodness, faithfulness, gentleness, self-control"* (Galatians 5:22–23).

Fasting accelerates death to the sinful nature. Therefore, in every fast you undertake, pay attention to how God is working to purify your soul and subjugate your flesh. When fasting becomes a regular part of your lifestyle, you will continually live in a place of death—but it is death to the old nature. So be glad! The life of Christ is becoming dominant in you and triumphing over the flesh!

Until the Holy Spirit and the life of God become our greatest reality, the flesh will dominate us.

Fasting Purifies Us from Negative Cycles and Patterns

Additionally, as we fast, God breaks us out of negative cycles and patterns in our emotions, thinking processes, will, and actions. You might be surprised to find what negative cycles have become established in your heart and life. (See, for example, Matthew 15:18–20.) These are not one-time or occasional problems but, rather, habitual ones. Some damaging patterns of thinking and behaving include anger, discouragement, depression, bitterness, strife, jealousy, doubt, unbelief, impure thoughts, fear, sadness, preoccupation with death, panic attacks, addictions, and sexual immorality.

We all have unhealthy patterns we need to let go of in order to become everything Christ redeemed us to be. What negative thought processes are you dealing with? Perhaps, every time someone says something to you like "You're no good," you fall into depression. Or, every time you have a fight in your family, you become discouraged and sad. Maybe you have mood swings or constantly deal with fear, insecurity, or jealousy. Perhaps you feel stuck in a pattern of financial predicaments, poverty, or broken relationships. You might feel you have done everything to overcome the situation, and nothing has changed. But have you fasted about it?

Cycles of negative behavior that reappear in our lives after we thought we were free of them can be especially distressing. For example, perhaps, at one point, you were delivered from pornography or addiction, yet after a period of time, you went back to living according to the old cycle. You wonder how that could have happened. Such harmful cycles must be broken through fasting and prayer.

In my own life, there have been certain cycles and patterns that I didn't like, and I told God that I wanted to break them. For example, I struggled with a pattern that happens with many preachers: Every time I had a great victory in ministry, either in the United States or abroad, I would somehow become discouraged, experiencing "the blues." I would pray, "God, I witnessed the blind receiving their sight and the deaf having their hearing restored, but now I feel discouraged." When I realized this was a regular cycle in my life, I said, "Wait a minute. Let me fast about this." And God set me free!

Do you want the negative behavior patterns in your life to change? Are you tired of being stuck in a destructive cycle? Mental and emotional patterns and bad habits can be broken during fasting. If you notice God bringing these patterns to your attention during a fast, don't become discouraged. He wants you to recognize that they are there, and then to yield to His cleansing work so you can be delivered from them. Your soul is being afflicted, but remember that your spirit is alive in Christ. The more of our problems we give to God, the more He will give of Himself to us.

In a related way, during a time of individual or corporate fasting, interpersonal problems that had remained buried or submerged—never having been dealt with—can begin to surface as God confronts us with our issues. I have seen open conflict erupt in families, churches, and even businesses when people have begun to fast. The work of Satan is exposed. People's good and bad motivations and intentions are uncovered. Their true hearts are revealed. For example, suppose there is someone you have harbored resentment against but have superficially tolerated in your interactions with them. Suddenly, in the middle of a fast, your resentment rises to the surface and you find yourself in an argument with that person. Be prepared for issues to surface, and continually seek God's forgiveness, healing, and reconciliation with others.

The purpose of fasting is to set you free, not to harm you.

Fasting Removes Stumbling Blocks

During fasting, God may also point out an area of our lives that is a stumbling block to us, even though it isn't a particular sin. For example, we may have personal preferences that, perhaps unknown to us, are interfering in our relationship with Him. It might be a romantic attachment, a superfluous activity, or a certain goal we've been pursuing. We can't allow any person, activity, or pursuit to become an idol to us. Anything that has become an idol to us, God will either remove or cause to be demoted in our life. To experience true, eternal life—right now, here on earth—we need more of God and less of us. That is why, as we consecrate ourselves to God, we make a decision to give up whatever is holding us back from Him.

When we fast, we commit to give more of ourselves to God and ask God for more of Himself. John the Baptist said of Jesus, *"He must increase, but I must decrease"* (John 3:30). Similarly, we can say, "I want the life of Christ to grow strong in me, but for that to happen, my 'self' must become less." As believers, we should want to lift up Jesus by our lives so that many people will come to know Him and receive His salvation and deliverance. Fasting is one of the quickest ways in which we can die to "self"—meaning our willfulness or desire to do things our own way rather than God's way. God has wonderful plans for us, but we hinder them because we think we know better than He does. Through fasting, we place our lives under submission to His lordship.

When God begins to confront us with various issues that need to be resolved, we may feel He is taking away some things that are important to us or have defined our lives to this point. However, the more He removes our issues and stumbling blocks, the more He gives of Himself and His blessings. The priorities of the temporal world will fade away from our sight, and the eternal kingdom of God will come into greater focus for us.

"He must increase, but I must decrease." Every time you fast, something of you will die, but something of Jesus will become alive in you as the Spirit takes over.

When fasting is part of your lifestyle, you will live in a place of continual death to self—and life in God.

Fasting Brings New Cycles, Patterns, and Seasons

Thus, the beginning of a fast does the work of fully capturing our attention so we will recognize our needs and allow God to remove the negative ways of thinking and behaving we have fallen into, including destructive patterns that need to be broken. Our soul might have been contaminated by ungodly spiritual atmospheres, or we might have gone back into living according to the flesh. We might be stuck in undesirable mental and emotional cycles, continually repeating the same patterns and mistakes without understanding how we became trapped in them.

Do you want change to occur in your life? Or do you want to repeat your old cycles and patterns of defeat? Unless you have a season of renewal, you will repeat those old cycles. Tell yourself, "No more damaging cycles in my life!" Initiate a fast by faith so that these negative cycles and patterns can be broken. Reach out to another believer or group of believers who can pray, fast, and stand with you until you receive deliverance.

When we fast, God not only sets us free from negative cycles and patterns, but He also releases us into new spiritual seasons and cycles of life. These are times of transformation, preparing us for what God wants to do next in our lives and the lives of others. You may have heard someone give a testimony such as, "I fasted, and God saved my family." As I emphasized earlier, this type of result is never a "payment" from God for fasting. It is because the heart of the person who fasted became aligned with God's heart, giving Him the freedom to move in their favor.

Our hearts must be prepared for the ways in which the Spirit is moving. For example, suppose God were to bring a large sum of money into your hands for the purpose of carrying out His will. If your heart isn't ready to receive it, having that money could lead you away from God instead of into His blessing and abundance. God wants you to be ready for His mega-blessings. That is why, if we want to enter a new dimension in a particular area of our life, such as our finances, we won't move into that new area unless we fast and seek God about it.

The more we fast, the more we will align our spirit with the life of God and the activity of heaven. If you want to be set free from contaminations, the desires of the flesh, and old patterns and cycles, and if you would like to enter into a new spiritual season, pray this prayer out loud:

> Heavenly Father, today, I ask You to show me any way in which my soul has been contaminated by an ungodly atmosphere. Then, cleanse me and restore me to You. I willingly crucify my flesh so that I may walk according

to Your Spirit. I acknowledge that I have negative and destructive patterns in my life—emotional, physical, mental, and spiritual. [Specifically name any that come to mind.] Deliver me from them all, purifying my soul and sharpening my spirit. Enable me to become sensitive to Your voice. Remove the blinders from my eyes that prevent me from discerning Your answers to the problems and crises in my life. Father, release a fresh anointing in me. I declare that this fast will take me into a new territory, a new season. In the name of Jesus, amen!

Testimonies of Breakthrough Fasts

My name is Priscilla Rodriguez. When I was twenty years old, I thought I would spend the rest of my life in jail. I had separated myself from the ways of God, and my life was very distorted. The things I was doing were leading to nothing but destruction. I was living a sinful life! Finding myself in jail, I started to fast for three days. While reading my Bible, God led me to a word that said, "My grace is sufficient; when you are weak, I am strong." (See 2 Corinthians 12:9–10.) As I went before the judge, I started declaring those words. After I had fasted and prayed for three days, on the day of the trial, I was cleared of all charges.

That day, I made a covenant with God that when I was set free, I would come to church and testify about His glory. In jail, God had allowed me to pray for other girls who were going through similar things as I was, and I am living proof of His goodness. I will spend the rest of my life ready to worship, dance, and praise Him for all He has done in my life.

6

INCREASING YOUR SPIRITUAL PERCEPTION

There are certain places and realms in the Spirit we won't have access to until our fasting and consecration to God open them up to us. For example, some people say they never hear God's voice in guidance or encouragement. What is the reason for this? God has prepared powerful blessings for them (as He has for all of us), but they haven't positioned themselves to be attuned to Him in order to receive that revelation. Others have received a word from God, but it is difficult for them to believe for its fulfillment because they haven't perceived in the Spirit what God wills and how He is working in the now.

For example, imagine you are in a crisis, and God wants to give you the solution for it. However, you can't see the answer because you're living according to the flesh, so your spiritual sight is veiled. Or, suppose you are headed in the wrong direction in life, hitting various "potholes" in your path. God wants you to be able to hear Him say, "You've been making some bad decisions—stop and listen to Me!" But your spiritual hearing is blocked by a negative pattern of depression, so you can't obtain what He is revealing to you.

Fasting and praying will not only open our spiritual perception, but they will also accelerate our ability to see and hear what God is communicating to us. What had previously been unclear or confusing to us—or leading us astray through deception—will become clear when God purifies our souls and we become accustomed to seeing and sensing in the spiritual dimension. Fasting can also enable us to perceive the root of a problem. Afterward, we say, "Why didn't I see this before? It's so obvious!" There have been times when I have sought God for something, but I was unable to receive it, even after spending much time in prayer. But when I engaged in a fast, I heard His voice and received the answer. Why couldn't I hear God beforehand? It was because my soul had not been cleansed and my spirit had not been sharpened. Fasting prepared me to discern and receive the answer I needed.

I hope you recognize the necessity and benefits of being cleansed from atmospheric contaminations, the fleshly nature, and negative patterns and cycles through fasting. God calls us to fasting and prayer so we can become focused on Him and see beyond the reach of our physical eyes. As we cease dwelling on the temporal reality of life's events and circumstances, we become more attuned to the greater reality of the spiritual domain. This enables us to take our eyes off of our lack, our sickness, or anything else that is outside of God's will. We enter a new season in which our level of spiritual sensitivity is raised. It becomes easier for us to discern the voice of God and learn His purposes and instructions for us—and to pray accordingly. Our prayers become more effective. We are able to receive divine strategies and creative ideas. We develop greater receptivity to the Spirit's movements. Thus, after God deals with various issues in our lives, He reveals Himself and His ways to us. We can perceive what He is saying about the situations we are going through and His overall purposes for our life.

The more spiritually attuned we become, the quicker we will perceive what is happening in the spiritual realm.

Three Kinds of Spiritual Vision

There are three kinds of spiritual vision we can experience as we consecrate ourselves to God in fasting. The first is "inner" vision, which is something you see in your mind's eye. The second is "open" vision, where you might see something in the physical atmosphere as if on a television screen. The third is "ecstasies." This is where you begin to see into the spiritual world, as in spiritual visions or "trances" (such as the apostle Peter experienced in Acts 10:9–16, or the apostle John experienced in the book of Revelation); in this type of vision, it is often as if you are in a state between being awake and being asleep.

Remember that, when He operated as a human being on earth, Jesus needed spiritual clarity in His mind and heart before confronting Satan in the wilderness (or anywhere else). However, Jesus prayed and fasted not only for spiritual strength to defeat the enemy but also to commune with the Father, receive revelation, and act on what was revealed to Him. For example, Jesus stated, *"Most assuredly, I say to you, the Son can do nothing of Himself, but* ***what He sees the Father do****; for whatever He does, the Son also does in like manner"* (John 5:19). God desires us to function in the same way—seeing what He is doing in the heavenly realm, and then doing the same thing on earth. He wants to work through us to bring what is in the eternal realm into the physical world as manifestations of His kingdom.

We see an excellent example of this process in the life of the prophet Jeremiah, who wrote,

> *Moreover the word of the Lord came to me, saying, "Jeremiah, what do you see?" And I said, "I see a branch of an almond tree." Then the Lord said to me, "You have seen well, for I am ready to perform My word ["I will hasten my word to perform it"* KJV]." (Jeremiah 1:11–12)

In answer to the Lord's question, *"Jeremiah, what do you see?"* the prophet replied, *"I see a branch of an almond tree."* Jeremiah's spiritual vision was sharp, and this enabled him to see into the spiritual realm to what God was doing. He saw what God saw. And the Lord told him, *"You have seen well, for I am ready to perform My word."* In the original Hebrew, the Lord's reply is essentially this: "Because you have seen well, I will accelerate and perform My word."

Today, God wants to make sure we, too, are seeing what He is seeing, so we can receive all that He has for us and be able to fulfill His purposes. I try my best to remain sharp in the Spirit, so I can receive God's revelations to me. For instance, sometimes, I am enabled to see when spiritual danger is coming and what I should do about it; other times, I am enabled to see what is truly going on in someone's life, beneath the surface, that is causing a particular problem. To minister effectively, I need to stay on the spiritual cutting edge. And fasting is an important way I maintain my position there.

Whenever we can see what God shows us, we are able to obey His will, receive His blessings, and walk in victory. When I was ready to buy the property where King Jesus Ministry now stands, I stepped onto the land, and I saw, in the Spirit, the building that would become the sanctuary, educational classrooms, counseling rooms, and more. What did I do? I started leaping! I started running and repeating, "I see it!" And God said, "Because you saw it, it's yours. I will accelerate it." He accelerated the process so that it was complete in under two and a half years. God will do the same for you—if you see something in the Spirit and accept it in faith, you will receive it, and God will accelerate the process.

To give you another example, I prayed for five years for God to do creative miracles, such as generating new organs and other body parts in people, because I felt that was included in my calling to minister the supernatural power of God. During that time, I saw a lot of healings—but not a lot of creative miracles. Then the Lord said to me, "Until you see them, I am not going to accelerate them." So I went into a fast, and, remarkably, I saw in the Spirit a woman's breast regrowing after having been surgically removed. God said, "You saw it; now I will accelerate it." Since then, I have seen many types of creative miracles in my ministry.

If you see something in the Spirit and accept it in faith, you will receive it, and God will accelerate the process.

What Do *You* See?

Many times, we obscure the answers to our prayers because we haven't sought God—fasting and consecrating our lives to Him—so we can see what He wants to show us, and then receive that revelation in faith. God tells us, in effect, "I was ready to give you the solutions to your questions and problems last week [or six months ago, or two years ago], but I haven't been able to get your attention. However, now you are fasting and praying, and you will be able to understand and receive My solutions for your marriage, your children, and your finances."

God has answers ready for you. Are *you* ready for them? Let me ask you: What do you see about your family? Your finances? Your school? Your crisis? God's condition for you to receive what you are waiting for, or His condition to accelerate your breakthrough, is that your spirit be sharp and focused on Him. God told Jeremiah, *"You have seen well"* (Jeremiah 1:12). It was as if He were saying, "Oh, Jeremiah, you have My attention, because you're seeing what I'm seeing, you're perceiving what I'm perceiving, you're hearing what I'm hearing." Similarly, God is telling us, "If you see and hear what I see and hear for your situation, this is what I will do."

Have you seen your miracle? Have you seen the healing for your body? Have you seen your house mortgage paid off? Acknowledge to God what He has revealed to you! For example, suppose, in the spiritual realm, you see your business growing, and then you tell God what you see; after that, you are able to sell a product you had a hard time selling before. Why? Because you saw it happen beforehand in the Spirit, and now it is being manifested in the physical world.

I believe there's an acceleration coming in your life! See it and rejoice!

Faith Has an Imagination

What if you still have difficulty seeing what God sees? You need to learn to walk by faith. "*For we walk by faith, not by* [physical] *sight*" (2 Corinthians 5:7). Living according to human reason can block your miracle. However, when you begin to live according to faith, you will learn that faith has an imagination that looks into the spiritual realm and perceives what you can't see in the physical world. This is what some people call a "sanctified imagination." Sometimes, we can't see what God sees because of our anxiety over present circumstances or our fear over what might happen in the future. Fear is a distortion of the imagination of God. When you fear, you imagine things that don't exist.

Yet, what you fear, you can attract and cause to manifest in the material world.

In contrast, when you see by faith, you see what is real in eternity, and that spiritual reality can be manifested on earth. For example, when you are praying, you might suddenly start seeing pictures of something. You think, *Why am I seeing these pictures? This is just my imagination.* But with spiritual vision, you experience God's imagination in you, not your own ideas. When God called me to minister, I received spiritual imaginations of big things—of preaching to people in large stadiums. At first, I thought I was crazy. I didn't know then that faith operates with imagination. However, God told me, "I'm showing you what is to come, because, if you can see it, I will hasten it."

Therefore, don't go by the bad news that you see, hear, and feel in the natural realm, but go by what God's Word says, and by what you perceive in the Spirit. If you see something, call it in! Say, "God, I am seeing something." You have to declare it. Then God will reply, "I will accelerate it." With spiritual sight, we can see that, in God, our breakthrough is on the way!

It is clear that you begin to see yourself by faith when you stop living according to your natural sight and senses and live according to the supernatural. When you walk only by sight and not by faith, there is no "super" connected with the natural, whether in regard to people, circumstances, or things. Thus, you end up walking slowly along the road of life—and stagnation sets in. But when the "super" is placed upon the natural, things accelerate!

If you want to open your spiritual sight and hearing as you fast and consecrate yourself to God, say the following prayer:.

> Father, I need You! I need Your guidance and instructions for my life. I need to know Your purposes for me and my family. Purify my soul and open my spiritual eyes and ears. Allow me to see what You see and to hear what You hear, so I can receive it in faith. Enable my spirit to be sensitive to the ways in which You are moving. Whatever I see and hear from You, I will declare! I know acceleration is coming upon my life. In Jesus's name, amen!

Now, allow me to pray for you:

> Father, in the name of the Lord Jesus Christ, remove from Your people's eyes any veil or cloud that is obscuring their spiritual sight, and any interference that is blocking their spiritual hearing. I release the anointing of deliverance, removing the blinders from their eyes and the blockage from their ears, so they can see and hear as You do, and so they can discern with a holy imagination what You have prepared for them. The hindrances are removed, right now, in the name of Jesus!

I encourage you to pray in the Holy Spirit, and when God shows you a solution or a blessing in the spiritual realm, say it out loud—declare it, and receive it!

Testimonies of Breakthrough Fasts

My name is Devin Perfumo. I grew up in a nice household, but when I was about ten, I found out that my parents were going to get divorced. My dad had developed a drinking problem, and whenever he would drink, he would also end up doing drugs, and my mother was fed up with it. She did not want her children growing up in that type of environment. When my parents first got divorced, it didn't bother me too much, but as the years progressed, not having a dad at home left me with a lot of empty time to wander around. I ended up becoming a street kid and playing in a band. I, too, began to develop a drinking problem that led me to take drugs—cocaine and ecstasy.

One day, when I saw all my friends around me getting high, I knew I'd had enough of that lifestyle. I fell to the floor of my room and cried out, "God, I don't know if You're real or not, but I need to know, because if this is life, I don't want to live another day. I need You to be real." A week later, an evangelist from King Jesus Ministry came up to me and said, "I don't know why, but I see you on the floor of your room. You cried out to God recently, and nobody else knows it." On top of that, he started telling me, "I see you playing music, I see you in a band, and I see you helping people who can't help you in return." At the time, I worked with autistic kids, and I was always doing programs with them. When the evangelist told me these things about myself, it shocked me.

I went to a service at the church, and there was a moment when it felt like a veil fell from my face; it felt like a hundred thousand pounds of weight fell off of me, and I began to cry. That's what really changed my life because I realized God is real. He isn't just a religion. He's an actual Being who speaks to us. He delights in fellowshipping and conversing with us. After that, I began to really experience the presence of God.

I started praying for my family, and, after I had been saved for a couple of years, I reached a point where I prayed, "God, if You saved me, You can save my family." One day, something happened with my dad, and I just got fed up. I made a covenant with the Lord that I wouldn't eat or drink anything until He did something in my father's life. My heart was set on this, and I prayed and worshipped as I went about my daily routines while fasting. A day and a half into the fast, the Holy Spirit told me I could eat again; He released me from the fast, and I knew that my prayer had been answered. A couple of hours later, I got a call that my father had been rushed to the hospital with severe stomach pains. The doctors and nurses were very concerned, saying that if my father's condition was what they thought it might be, then he might not live another day. My father was going in and out of consciousness, and he was scared. But I remember feeling the Holy Spirit with me the whole time. It was clear to me that what was happening was a result of what I had prayed for and put a claim on God to do.

My dad's condition stabilized, and a couple of days later, he was discharged from the hospital. I learned that as he lay in his hospital bed, he made a covenant with God that if he lived, he would stop doing drugs and drinking alcohol. Now, two and a half years later, I can testify that my father is still clean; he hasn't smoked weed, taken cocaine, or consumed alcohol. He became a Christian, and he has been attending church. He frequently calls me to pray with him; in fact, we're always praying together.

If God hadn't revealed to me His heart in prayer and intimacy, I never would have known His plans for my family. But because He did, I knew how to pray, seek, and push in the Spirit for my family. I knew how to hear God's voice for them. Now they're saved and have encountered God. My family, which used to lead people into the things of the world, now leads people into the things of God!

7

FASTING PROVOKES BREAKTHROUGH

Throughout this book, we have seen a number of ways in which fasting appropriates the presence, power, and blessings of God. In this chapter, I want to focus on some of the most challenging and entrenched issues—whether spiritual, mental, emotional, or physical—in which fasting is necessary for breakthrough.

Demonic Forces Operating in the World

As noted earlier, the second coming of the Lord is drawing near, and thus Satan has released powerful evil spirits on the earth to bring confusion and destruction in the world and to attack believers. We are now dealing with high-ranking demonic beings that we have never seen before. Among these entities are spirits of antichrist, sexual immorality, rebellion, lawlessness, witchcraft, occultism, false religion, oppression, intellectualism, and more. These spirits know they don't have much time left before their judgment by God, so they are out tracking the earth, hindering millions of believers, putting limitations and barriers on them to block their advancement in the kingdom. Many Christians are dealing with crises, overwhelming circumstances, and mountainous problems, and they desperately need breakthroughs.

Remember, a breakthrough is a sudden spiritual burst that pushes us beyond our limitations and into deliverance and freedom. Unless we pray and fast, we cannot win the victory over these satanic attacks. We have to fight against them in the Spirit. As we fast and commune with God, He will put deposits of power in our life to enable us to receive breakthroughs.

High-ranking, demonic spirits are not defeated without prayer and fasting.

Prayer and Fasting as a Spiritual Weapon

Jesus taught that fasting, in combination with prayer, is a spiritual weapon for dealing with powerful demonic spirits. It is important to read the following passage in its entirety because we will be looking at key principles from it.

> *And when they* [Jesus, along with Peter, James, and John] *had come to the multitude, a man came to Him, kneeling down to Him and saying, "Lord, have mercy on my son, for he is an epileptic and suffers severely; for he often falls into the fire and often into the water. So I brought him to Your* [other] *disciples, but they could not cure him." Then*

> *Jesus answered and said, "O faithless and perverse generation, how long shall I be with you? How long shall I bear with you? Bring him here to Me." And Jesus rebuked the demon, and it came out of him; and the child was cured from that very hour. Then the disciples came to Jesus privately and said, "Why could we not cast it out?" So Jesus said to them, "Because of your unbelief; for assuredly, I say to you, if you have faith as a mustard seed, you will say to this mountain, 'Move from here to there,' and it will move; and nothing will be impossible for you. However, this kind does not go out except by prayer and fasting."*
>
> (Matthew 17:14–21)

There are some things in your life that you can pray about and obtain victory over fairly easily. Then there are other situations that are so tough, they don't respond to ordinary means, such as "regular" prayer, counseling, or the skills of doctors. To overcome the kind of demonic opposition Jesus was talking about, which has developed roots and has become a stronghold, we need increased power in the Spirit.

Authority Versus Power

Notice that the deliverance of the demonized boy happened instantly, in the now: *"the child was cured from that very hour"* (Matthew 17:18). Jesus was able to immediately expel the demon because He had a lifestyle of fasting and prayer. As we read in Matthew 10:1, before this incident, Jesus had already given His disciples authority in His name to cast out demons. The word *"power"* in that verse refers to "the right to exercise power." This is the same authority Jesus has given the church: *"And these signs will follow those who believe: in My name they will cast out demons..."* (Mark 16:17). The expression *"in My name"* signifies "in the power of My name," "in the authority of My name," or "on My behalf."

In the power of their delegated authority from Jesus, the disciples had been able to cast out demons—until they came up against this case they could not handle. When they asked Jesus why they hadn't been successful in bringing deliverance, He answered:

> *Because of your unbelief; for assuredly, I say to you, if you have faith as a mustard seed, you will say to this mountain, "Move from here to there," and it will move; and nothing will be impossible for you.* ***However, this kind does not go out except by prayer and fasting.***
>
> (Matthew 17:20–21; see also Mark 9:29)

Jesus said there is only one way to expel *"this kind"*—a certain demonic entity; there is only one way to move this type of mountain. Not two or three ways, but *one way:* prayer and fasting. Only the spiritual weapon of fasting, in conjunction with prayer, could effectively deal with it.

The disciples had authority, but they did not have sufficient power to cast out the demonic spirit. That took prayer and fasting. Likewise, in order to exercise spiritual authority, we must have the power to back it up. If not, our authority is meaningless.

And fasting is the place where we can legally obtain and increase supernatural power in our lives to carry out the authority Jesus has given us.

There was an incident in the ministry of Paul in which he was confronted by an evil spirit in a slave girl, but he did not immediately cast out that spirit. He waited days before doing so. I believe he may have been fasting during that time for spiritual power to defeat the demon.

> *Now it happened, as we went to prayer, that a certain slave girl possessed with a spirit of divination met us, who brought her masters much profit by fortune-telling. This girl followed Paul and us, and cried out, saying, "These men are the servants of the Most High God, who proclaim to us the way of salvation." And this she did for many days. But Paul, greatly annoyed, turned and said to the spirit, "I command you in the name of Jesus Christ to come out of her." And he came out that very hour.* (Acts 16:16–18)

Sometimes, people will try to cast out an evil spirit, but the spirit does not leave because it recognizes they lack authority and power to command it. When this occurs, a demon may turn on those trying to cast it out. This happened to the sons of Sceva in the book of Acts. (See Acts 19:14–16.) In that situation, although the demon did not acknowledge the authority of these sons of Sceva, it did readily acknowledge the authority of Jesus—and of Paul, who was exercising authority and power in Jesus's name. When we are acting fully under Jesus's authority and the power of the Spirit, then strong demons, or "*principalities and powers*" (Colossians 2:15; see also Ephesians 6:12), will recognize our voice of authority; we will have credibility with them, and they will have to obey us. We can say to someone who is possessed by a demon, "Be set free!" and they will be delivered. We can declare to someone who is ill, "Be healed!" and the sickness will leave. We can command a demonic obstacle, "Be removed, now, in Jesus's name!" and it will get out of our way.

In order to exercise spiritual authority, we must have the power to back it up.

Long-Standing Issues

In a parallel account of the demonized boy from Mark's gospel, Jesus asked the child's father, "'*How long has this been happening to him?' And he said, 'From childhood*'" (Mark 9:21). I believe Jesus asked the history of this case because He wanted to discover the demon's entry point and longevity in the child's life. We don't know boy's age, but we do know that the spirit had been oppressing him for many years, perhaps since the time he was born, or maybe even while he was still in his mother's womb. That is why the demon was so strong and entrenched.

If given the opportunity, the enemy will establish roots in people's lives. Whenever a demonic entity establishes a root, it becomes a stronghold. In the natural world, a stronghold is defined as "a place that has been fortified so as to protect it against attack." Strongholds are not easily removed; it takes a great amount of force to do so. Likewise, in the spiritual world, it takes increased supernatural power to demolish entrenched strongholds. The stronghold might be doubt, idolatry, rebellion, or a religious spirit. It might be sexual deviation or a gambling addiction. It might be a generational curse, which is an issue that is passed down through succeeding generations, so that a person's children and grandchildren are afflicted by the same malady they struggled with.

If you are dealing with a long-standing problem with which you or someone else has been afflicted for five, ten, twenty, thirty—even forty or more—years, then you must obtain increased power through fasting to destroy its deep roots. It may take a longer period of fasting for the issue to be resolved.

Today, Jesus is asking us, as He asked the father of the demonized boy, "*How long...?*" He doesn't ask us this question to gain information, because He already knows the answer. Instead, it is to help us see the depth of our need. He is asking, "How long have you had this disease? How long have you had this financial problem? How long have you had this depression? How long have you had this sexual issue? How long have you had these panic attacks?" If it is a long time, you need to recognize that there are likely negative spiritual roots present. You must be able to rebuke them in the power of the Spirit in order to be set free.

Do you need a breakthrough now? Is anything limiting or constraining you? Is something hindering you from moving forward? Is your body afflicted? Are you in the middle of spiritual warfare? Are you facing a crisis in your mind or emotions? Do you need a miracle? I believe this is the time for you to proclaim a fast in faith. Your spirit needs to be expanded, through fasting, to act in a higher capacity, in order to birth extreme and unusual victory in the spiritual realm to overcome the powerful demonic forces at work.

Your spirit needs to be expanded, through fasting, to act in a higher capacity, in order to birth extreme and unusual victory in the spiritual realm.

Moving Mountains

Jesus said that if we have faith, we can move mountains. However, some mountains take more than just faith to be moved—they necessitate prayer and fasting. (See Matthew 17:20–21.) When the enemy places a mountain in our path, it is for the purpose of halting the advancement of God's kingdom and God's children. A mountain can represent something that blocks the way for you to hear God's guidance, receive healing, fulfill your purpose, or anything else. Sometimes, this takes the form of a "spirit of delay." A biblical example of this is when the prophet Daniel humbled himself and engaged in a partial fast for twenty-one days, and experienced a spirit of delay (called the "*prince of Persia*") before receiving his answer. (See Daniel 10.)

Today, demonic spirits of delay are causing the holdup of many answers and blessings that God wants to give us. We must humble ourselves and begin to fast and pray, waging war against these spirits—the entities responsible for the delay of our family's salvation, our financial prosperity, the development of our ministry, and other purposes of God. When we seek God's face through fasting and prayer, He wages war on our behalf. Thus, if the enemy is blocking or delaying an area of your life, declare a fast and *allow God to fight for you.* Speak to the principality in the name of Jesus and order it to release your blessings!

Appropriate the Power!

Often, people who are facing demonic strongholds or other difficult situations want their pastor or another leader in the church to pray for them to bring deliverance. It is good for spiritual leaders to be involved in deliverance, and sometimes people are so deeply afflicted they can't do it on their own. But it's essential to understand that every believer has the right to pray and fast for deliverance when dealing with demonic attack and oppression. Often, one of the requirements for receiving a breakthrough is that we become fed up with the issue, problem, or crisis. If you are complacent about your sickness, financial problem, absence of peace, or stagnant spiritual condition, then breakthrough will not come. You need to deny your flesh, declare a fast, and receive the victory. Decide, "I am going to remove every mountain from my life!" You will be able to remove entrenched demonic oppression because you already have the authority in Christ—and you will receive the necessary increase in supernatural power by fasting.

Let us receive what God offers us and not take His presence and power in our lives lightly. Instead of remaining in our needs, sicknesses, and oppressions, we must make a conscious decision to receive what Christ has won for us by appropriating His power. Now is the time to press through to breakthrough by prayer and fasting! There is always someone "crazy in faith" who reaches out for God's power and deliverance, like the woman who suffered from the issue of blood for twelve years, but then reached out to touch the hem of Jesus's garment and received her healing. (See, for example, Matthew 9:20–22.) There are certain people in my congregation who always receive from God when they come to services because they don't come casually; they come ready to appropriate all of God's blessings.

Don't wait for someone else to obtain your breakthrough! Begin by praying this prayer:

> Father, in the name of Jesus, release upon me the desire to fast in order to receive the power I need to overcome the attacks of high-level demonic entities and long-standing issues whose roots have grown deep in my life. Cover me with the blood of Jesus for protection and victory against the enemy. In Jesus's name, amen!

Now, I want to speak this declaration over your life:

> I come into agreement with you that every demonic attack and long-standing issue in your life is broken. I demolish every stronghold in your mind, emotions, family, finances, or any other area. I break every generational curse and every entrenched problem of sexual

immorality, alcoholism, poverty, fear, depression, witchcraft, illness, or anything else—now, in Jesus's name!

Today, walk in God's power and authority, and receive your deliverance. Chains are being broken, and mountains are being removed, right now. As you are set free, deliver others as you have been delivered. Stir up the gifts and anointing within you through the Holy Spirit—to heal the sick, cast out demons, and raise the dead, in the name of Jesus. Amen and amen!

Testimonies of Breakthrough Fasts

Darlise Jackson had been in remission from cancer for two years, but then the cancer returned, and she had malignant tumors in her breast. The Lord led her to fast, and she fasted, prayed, and gave offerings. Here is her testimony:

> I was diagnosed with cancer in 2014, and after I underwent chemotherapy, the doctors said the cancer was gone. However, the chemotherapy had made me sick. The aftereffects were horrible, and it had taken a toll on my body. Then I started attending King Jesus Ministry, arriving about the time the Apostolic and Prophetic Conference was taking place. I decided to read through Apostle Maldonado's books, and I came to a place where I read, "Jesus heals your sickness today." This was significant for me because the doctors soon told me the cancer had returned, and I needed to go back on chemotherapy. I received the treatment, but it didn't work,

and two weeks later, I was told I needed to have another round of chemotherapy. I really wanted to be healed, but I wanted the Lord to heal me, and I was not willing to compromise my healing by having the chemotherapy. That week, I praised God as much as I could, and I also worshipped Him. During worship, the Holy Spirit took over, and I began to sob in His presence. I couldn't stop weeping, and I began to cry out to God. Soon afterward, I checked my breast but couldn't feel any tumors there. I went to the doctor, and it was confirmed—the cancer was gone!

8

PRACTICAL STEPS TO FASTING

We must personally receive—as revelation—the necessity, the why, and the how of fasting; otherwise, we won't practice it. Has something stirred in your spirit as you've read this book? Have you received the Scriptures and principles on fasting as a personal revelation? Will you commit to making fasting a lifestyle in order to seek God's face, live in His presence, be on the front lines of the move of the Holy Spirit, and walk in His power?

To help you in that commitment, I want to give you some practical steps to fasting in faith. I have been in ministry for more than twenty-five years, and because fasting has become a lifestyle for me, the recommendations I give you do not come from head knowledge alone but from my experience in seeing the power of spiritual fasting in my life and others' lives.

Steps to Fasting Effectively

1. Ask the Holy Spirit to Give You a Hunger to Fast

First, ask the Holy Spirit to release within you a hunger to fast and a desire to make fasting a lifestyle rather than just an "event" that you do every year—or every five or ten years when you face a crisis.

2. Determine the Purpose(s) of the Fast

Determine the specific reason or reasons for the fast you will undertake. There is reward in fasting, so be specific about what you are asking God to do for you. (See Matthew 6:18.) Then let Him work according to His purposes. For example, the reason for your fast may be to draw closer to God in greater intimacy and to spend extra time worshipping and praising Him. It may be for someone's salvation, physical healing, or freedom from bondage. It may be for guidance and direction for your life, family, and ministry. It may be for wisdom in a crisis. It may be for discernment for a business proposal or relationship. I encourage you to write down your expectations. Remember, when we don't expect, our faith is not active. We have to expect to receive.

3. Choose the Type of Fast

Choose the type of fast you will engage in: partial or total. Also choose its length: one meal, a full day, three days, one week, three weeks, or any other time that you have decided on.

4. Prepare Your Body for Fasting

Prepare your body two or three days prior to beginning the fast by eating less than usual.

5. Declare the Fast Before God and Receive Your Reward Now

Although you have already determined the purpose and length of your fast, declare it out loud to God. For example, you can say:

> Father, in the name of Jesus, I come before You and proclaim this [one-day, three-day, one-week, or other length], [partial or total] fast. I give this time to You, so I can draw nearer to You. I declare that the purpose of my fast is to [name the purpose]. I declare that as I fast, false patterns of thinking and negative emotional and behavioral cycles are broken in my life. My spiritual perception is sharp and more attuned to You. I hear, see, and perceive in the Spirit with precision. I receive Your grace and anointing, and the flow of the supernatural is sustained in me. I proclaim that this fast stirs up and increases the gifts of the Spirit in my life. I appropriate supernatural power now to destroy roots and strongholds, and I declare breakthrough in every area of my life. In Jesus's name, amen!

Additionally, Jesus said, "*Your Father who sees* [your fasting] *in secret will reward you openly*" (Matthew 6:18), and "*Therefore I say to you, whatever things you ask when you pray, believe that you receive them, and you will have them*" (Mark 11:24). Therefore, make a point to thank God beforehand for the reward of the fast: "Lord, in faith, I receive Your blessings and rewards now."

6. Spend Quality Time with God

During your fast, spend quality time alone with God as much as possible. Worship the Lord; pray; read, study, and meditate on the Word; listen to recorded teachings and praise music; and read Christian teaching and inspirational books. As you seek God, the Holy Spirit will reveal to you more of the Father, more of Jesus, more of the meaning of the cross, and more of the truth of the Scriptures. This is a special opportunity for communion and union with God. Make the time for it!

7. Present Your Body to God as a Living Sacrifice

As a priest before God, actively present your body to Him as a living sacrifice. You can pray:

> Lord, I am exercising one of the sacrifices of a priest of the new covenant by presenting my body as a living sacrifice before You. I die to "self." I die to what I want, what I feel, and what I think, so that the will and mind of Jesus will rule in me. Let this fast accelerate my death to self, so that I will decrease, and Your life in me will increase. I crucify my flesh and yield to Your cleansing process, so that my spirit can rule over my soul and body, and I can fulfill Your purposes for my life. In Jesus's name, amen.

8. Ask the Holy Spirit to Release His Supernatural Grace

Paul wrote, *"For many walk, of whom I have told you often, and now tell you even weeping, that they are the enemies of the cross of Christ: whose end is destruction, whose god is their belly, and whose glory is in their shame—who set their mind on earthly things"* (Philippians 3:18–19). The flesh will present us with many excuses for why we can't fast. It is constantly focusing on earthly matters and fighting against the cross—meaning the self-denial and self-sacrifice needed for victory. The flesh doesn't want to sacrifice, go the extra mile, or obey God's will.

Accordingly, keep in mind that the first few days of fasting are usually difficult, even if you have practiced fasting for a while. Although I fast regularly, I still find those beginning days of fasting by faith to be hard. My flesh says, "Please, just give me a little sugar to keep me going!" In the past, I have tried to fast in my own ability, and it didn't work. I needed God's grace to see it through.

Grace is given to the humble, and it is received by faith. As we humble ourselves, God enables us to persevere in fasting. (See James 4:6.) Supernatural grace gives us the ability to do what we can't do in our own strength, and to be what we can't be on our own. For example, suppose you say you're going to fast but then end up eating. You will likely feel guilty and want to pull away from the Lord. However, if that happens, just tell Jesus you are sorry and ask for His supernatural grace. Tell Him you can't fast in your own ability: "Lord, You know that I want to eat my favorite foods today. I ask You to give me an anointing of Your supernatural grace so that I won't eat. Please remove the hunger from me and help me to focus on the purpose of this fast." In the meantime, be sure to stay away, as much as possible, from places where you can see and smell food; don't put yourself in a position where you will be tempted to eat or drink something you have purposed to abstain from for your fast.

Also, remember that, in a sovereign fast, God will often remove your appetite when He prompts you to begin to fast. One time, He called me to go on a twenty-one-day fast to release a resurrection anointing in my ministry, and I found the fast to be easy for me. Why? Because, when God calls you to fast, He gives you the supernatural grace to do it in the strength of the Holy Spirit. Therefore, maintain intimacy with the Father through prayer, and ask for His help. He will empower you to do what you cannot do on your own.

9. Eliminate Distractions

Fasting is a time of consecration and separation to God in order to seek His face. As I noted earlier, the enemy knows your fast will bring a breakthrough in your life or others' lives, so he will bring distractions and temptations to try to get you to lose your focus and stop fasting. Therefore, remove or stay away from diversions that will hinder your intimacy with God; for example, avoid watching television, surfing the Internet, and logging on to social media. Turn off your telephone during times of prayer. Put a temporary hold on your social life.

10. Expect Some Physical and Emotional Symptoms

Expect certain physical and emotional symptoms to arise. As accumulated toxins and fat in your body are eliminated, you will likely experience headaches, body aches, bad breath, and perhaps even vomiting. When these symptoms appear, it is usually a sign that the body is cleansing itself. Additionally, you may feel tired or irritable. Ask the Holy Spirit to help you endure. It's likely these symptoms will last only one to three days.

Perhaps you have fasted before, and you have struggled to give up coffee, for example, during that time because you get headaches. As for me, I don't want any type of food or drink to be my master—only Jesus. That is part of my consecration to Him. As mentioned above, in such situations, you can admit your need to God and receive His grace to see you through.

11. Exercise the Full Fast

It is obvious that spiritual fasting is not just a physical act but has much deeper significance. This is clearly expressed by God through the prophet Isaiah in the following passage:

> *Is this not the fast that I have chosen: to loose the bonds of wickedness, to undo the heavy burdens, to let the oppressed go free, and that you break every yoke? Is it not to share your bread with the hungry, and that you bring to your house the poor who are cast out; when you see the naked, that you cover him, and not hide yourself from your own flesh?*
>
> (Isaiah 58:6–7)

As you fast, think of the needs of others, as well as yourself. Fulfill your responsibilities to your family, give to the needy, deliver the oppressed, offer hope to the discouraged, and encourage the fearful.

Fasting helps give us an increased awareness of other people's needs. Moreover, only when we've discerned, through prayer, the issues and difficulties of our generation can we fully consecrate ourselves to God to be used to minister to these needs. And, without the power of God, it is impossible to solve the problems of humanity. The current generation needs God desperately but lacks the power to overcome its many issues. During your fast, ask God to show you the big picture of His purposes for the world: the people in this generation need to know God and consecrate themselves to Him! Once more, ask God to release in you a hunger to fast, so that you can advance in your Christian walk, bringing the good news of the gospel of Jesus Christ to others and carrying healing and deliverance wherever you go!

12. Prepare to Come Out of the Fast

At the conclusion of your fast, avoid rich foods that might upset your stomach. It is wise to introduce small amounts of light foods to the body, a little at a time, beginning with fruit, such as grapes, bananas, and melons, which are easily digestible. This precaution is necessary, especially after longer fasts, because after a fast, the enzymes in our bodies are not immediately prepared to process solid food.

Although our priority when fasting is always to seek God's presence, in the process, we can see a difference in our body, our spirit, and our soul. For example, as mentioned earlier, depending on the length of the fast, our body may be cleansed of unhealthy and dangerous toxins. We may experience weight loss. Although that is not the reason for spiritual fasting, it is a positive outcome for many people, making them feel better, improving their body's performance, and reducing the harmful effects of obesity. As a result of detoxification, our attitudes and emotions can radically improve. Fasting also strengthens our "*inner man.*" (See Ephesians 3:16–17.) Once our emotions are under submission to the Spirit, they become more stable, and we are enabled to live at a greater level of anointing. And because the flesh is placed under subjection, it becomes easier for us to live in the Spirit.

Make Fasting Your Lifestyle

As I emphasized at the beginning of this book, these are "*times of restoration*" (Acts 3:21). God is calling His people to return to fasting, praying, and seeking His face. Decide today to make prayer and fasting a lifestyle for you by making this declaration:

> I present my body before God as a living and holy sacrifice, through fasting and prayer. I choose to pray and fast as a lifestyle.

ABOUT THE AUTHOR

Apostle Guillermo Maldonado is the senior pastor and founder of King Jesus International Ministry (Ministerio Internacional El Rey Jesus), in Miami, Florida, a multicultural church considered to be one of the fastest growing in the United States. King Jesus Ministry, whose foundation is built upon the Word of God, prayer, and worship, currently has a membership of nearly seventeen thousand. Apostle Maldonado is a spiritual father to more than 330 churches in 50 countries throughout the United States, Latin America, Europe, Africa, Asia, and New Zealand, which form the Supernatural Movement Network (formerly called the New Wine Apostolic Network), representing over six hundred thousand people. He is also the founder of the University of the Supernatural Ministry (USM). The building of kingdom leaders and the visible manifestations of God's supernatural power distinguish the ministry as the number of its members constantly multiplies.

A national best-selling author, Apostle Maldonado has written over fifty books and manuals, many of which have been translated into other languages. His books with Whitaker House include *Breakthrough Prayer, How to Walk in the Supernatural Power of God, The Glory of God, The Kingdom of Power, Supernatural Transformation, Supernatural Deliverance,* and *Divine Encounter with the Holy Spirit,* all of which are available in both English and Spanish. In addition, he preaches the message of Jesus Christ and His redemptive power on his international television program, *The Supernatural Now* (*Lo sobrenatural ahora*), which airs on TBN, Daystar, the Church Channel, and fifty other networks, with a potential outreach and impact to more than two billion people around the world.

Apostle Maldonado has a doctorate in Christian counseling from Vision International University and a master's degree in practical theology from Oral Roberts University. He resides in Miami, Florida, with his wife and ministry partner, Ana, and their two sons, Bryan and Ronald.